Deconstruction and Theology

Deconstruction and Theology

THOMAS J. J. ALTIZER · MAX A. MYERS
CARL A. RASCHKE · ROBERT P. SCHARLEMANN
MARK C. TAYLOR · CHARLES E. WINQUIST

CROSSROAD · NEW YORK

To Yog Satoth

1982

The Crossroad Publishing Company
575 Lexington Avenue, New York, NY 10022

Printed in the United States of America

LIBRARY OF CONGRESS CATALOGING IN PUBLICATION DATA

Main entry under title:

Deconstruction and theology.

    1. Theology—20th century—Addresses, essays,
lectures. I. Altizer, Thomas J. J.
BT28.D38   230   82-1377
ISBN 0-8245-0475-5   AACR2
ISBN 0-8245-0412-7 (pbk.)

Contents

We knowers are unknown to ourselves, and for a good reason: how can we ever hope to find what we have never looked for?

FRIEDRICH NIETZSCHE

Preface

Not too long ago an editor for a nationally known book publisher commented in a strangely impassive tone of voice that "no one reads theology anymore." His hyperbole aside, the remark ought to be taken seriously, although not with the expected hand-wringings, academic self-analysis, and ceremonial *mea culpa*. Perhaps "no one" reads theology anymore, because what we generally understand as theological discourse has exhausted its semantic capital, its power to generate a plausible system of reference. Perhaps we have genuinely arrived at the era that will be remembered as "the end of theology." Such a recognition should in itself be a cause for rejoicing, as at the close of graduation day when one pulls off one's cap and gown. Distress, anxiety, and malaise can only be interpreted during such an epochal transition as psychosomatic repercussions felt by those who have not learned to draw a candid distinction between loyalty to a field or a "tradition" and professional self-interest. An affective equilibrium is best struck by a therapeutic delight in abetting the necessary, historical demolition. It is edifying to recall Nietzsche's suggestion that we give a robust shove to what is already toppling. To swing a wrecking ball, once the edifice has been condemned and is uninhabitable, is more blessed than to launch pious protests. The death of theology's God should not be addressed in the same way as the death of Calvin Coolidge, when it was politely asked: "How do they know?" Hence deconstruction!

What is deconstruction? The term has already gained an *au courant* status in literary and philosophical circles, but it remains to enter into a fateful liaison with the practitioners of "theological" inquiry. Suffice it to say that deconstruction is neither a subject matter nor a methodology; for both presuppose a kind of unreflective integrity, or pristine utility, as regards language. There is no language of deconstruction, no "grammar" for second-order deliberations, no occasion for metacriticism. Deconstruction does not dwell within any special language, because it is the consummatory, apocalyptic movement *inside* Western thought and discourse; it does not subvert in a transitive sense the language of theology and metaphysics, because it is the movement and moment of that language's own self-subversion. If deconstruction is branded as nihilistic, it should be noted that it does nought but reveal the inherent nihilism of its host discipline. Where the body is, there shall the eagles gather. It is fitting today that deconstruction should spread throughout the corpus (or "corpse") of theology, because the theological mind has been responsible for the modern elevation of the linguistic signifier, which Derrida's "play of difference" exposes as a phantom, a veiled abyss, a nothingness. In Derrida's words: "the age of the sign is essentially theological."

The following collection of essays is not *about* deconstruction. Such folderol should be reserved for librarians, journalists, and intellectual voyeurs. In different measures each *is* an act of deconstruction, while *incorporating* some didactic content as to the genesis, function, and prospect of the "deconstructionist" movement. For the record, we can say that deconstruction has its gallery of Gothic-faced pioneers and palladins: Nietzsche, Heidegger, Derrida, Deleuze, Foucault, Rorty. But these are only proper names stenciled on the prow of writing which, as Derrida puts it, marks the "end of the book and the beginning of the text." My own essay, "The Deconstruction of God," launches the adventure by thinking through the antecedents, mentors, motives, and intimations of a future civilized madness in the deconstructionist movement, with special attention to the varieties of theological vanity. Winquist's "Body, Text, and Imagination," following Julia Kristeva, charts the way in which theology must look into its own glass and grasp how it has been embedded in a semantics of repression, then recapture the "economics of force" and the rhythms of desire. Taylor's "Text as Victim" shows how textuality is the final meaning of the incarnate Word, where logos is no longer transcendent, but "sacrificed" and totally "disseminated." The next two essays by Scharlemann ("The Being of God When God Is Not Being God") and Myers ("Toward What Is Religious Thinking Underway?") bring to the fore the import of Heidegger's program in the undertaking of theological deconstruction. Finally, Altizer's "History as Apocalypse," with typical rhetorical and poetic dash, brings down the curtain by underscoring how deconstruction is not merely a new brand of "critical" insight nor simply demythologizing, but the "end" of historical consciousness. This end is God's eschatological self-embodiment, which effaces the theological task.

. . . *dies illa, solvet saeculum in favilla.*

CARL A. RASCHKE

I

CARL A. RASCHKE

The Deconstruction of God

The madman—Have you not heard of that madman who lit a lantern in the bright morning hours, ran to the market place, and cried incessantly: "I seek God! I seek God!"—As many of those who did not believe in God were standing around just then, he provoked much laughter. Has he got lost? asked one. Did he lose his way like a child? asked another. Or is he hiding? Is he afraid of us? Has he gone on a voyage? emigrated?—Thus they yelled and laughed.

The madman jumped into their midst and pierced them with his eyes. "Whither is God?" he cried; "I will tell you. *We have killed him*—you and I. All of us are his murderers. But how did we do this? How could we drink up the sea? Who gave us the sponge to wipe away the entire horizon? What were we doing when we unchained this earth from its sun? Whither is it moving now? Whither are we moving? Away from all suns? Are we not plunging continually? Backward, sideward, forward, in all directions? Is there still any up or down? Are we not straying as through an infinite nothing? Do we not feel the breath of empty space? Has it not become colder? Is not night continually closing in on us? Do we not need to light lanterns in the morning? Do we hear nothing as yet of the noise of the gravediggers who are burying God? Do we smell nothing as yet of the divine decomposition? Gods, too, decompose. God is dead. God remains dead. And we have killed him.

"How shall we comfort ourselves, the murderers of all murderers? What was holiest and mightiest of all that the world has yet owned has bled to death under our knives: who will wipe this blood off us? What water is there for us to clean ourselves? What festivals of atonement, what sacred games shall we have to invent? Is not the greatness of this deed too great for us? Must we ourselves not become gods simply to appear worthy of it? There has never been a greater deed; and whoever is born after us—for the sake of this deed he will belong to a higher history than all history hitherto."

Here the madman fell silent and looked again at his listeners; and they, too, were silent and stared at him in astonishment. At last he threw his lantern on the ground, and it broke into pieces and went out. "I have come too early," he said then; "my time is not yet. This tremendous event is still on its way, still wandering; it has not yet reached the ears of men. Lightning and thunder require time; the light of the stars requires time; deeds, though done, still require time to be seen and heard. This deed is still more distant from them than the most distant stars—*and yet they have done it them-selves.*"

It has been related further that on the same day the madman forced his way into several churches and there struck up his *requiem aeternam deo.* Led out and called to account, he is said always to have replied nothing but: "What after all are these churches now if they are not the tombs and sepulchers of God?"

FRIEDRICH NIETZSCHE, *The Gay Science*

I

The word *deconstruction* has now overlapped fashionable literary precincts and implanted itself in the theological lexicon. Deconstruction in theology, however, does not signal a new "trend" among theologians akin to those wearisome fads and mannerisms celebrated among clerics and religious writers during the past two decades. Deconstruction is not a development, but a *movement.* Furthermore, it does not constitute a movement in religious thinking or the humanities *intra se,* but in Western culture as a whole. Deconstruction is the revelation of the inner vacuity of the much touted "modern" outlook; it is the saying, not straightaway but by the method of indirection, what has remained the jealously guarded secret of contemporary theological pedants as well as the high priests of "post-Christian" civilization, namely, that the idols of the secular marketplace have a tinny ring. Deconstruction shows that the logos of all our latter-day "——ologies," including theology, has become nought but a ritualistic and compulsive defense against *to kenon* ("the void"). What was heretofore a doxology is now a muttering in the dark. The hallelujahs of Easter sunrise have faded into a perplexity before the empty tomb. Theology assumes as principal charge the *composition of epitaphs.* Deconstruction, which must be considered the interior drive of twentieth-century theology rather than an alien agenda, is in the final analysis *the death of God put into writing,* the subsumption of the "Word" by the "flesh," the deluge of immanence. Deconstruction, therefore, traces the closing circle of "nihilism" which Nietzsche, our major prophet of modernity, glimpsed as the "strangest of guests" loitering by the door while the house collapses.

From the standpoint of late twentieth-century intellectual history, the roots of deconstruction lie in what might be regarded as a spontaneous revolt against the liberal orthodoxies of postwar philosophy and theology. Among these orthodoxies two stand in relief: linguistic formalism and anthropological reductionism. The attack on linguistic formalism had been led by the French philosopher Jacques Derrida, who has coined the term *deconstruction,* and his American counterpart Richard Rorty, who, in his recent controversial book *Philosophy and the Mirror of Nature,* assails the cumulative Anglo-American tradition of positivism and logical analysis.[1] The brief against anthropological reductionism has been made by the philosopher-historian Michel Foucault, who suggests that the ongoing modern wish to think through all issues of substance within the framework of ideological humanism is but a vanity spun from an illusion. The illusion is that "man," the prominent subject matter for all systematic "anthropological" inquiry, exists in any other fashion than what Foucault calls a "discursive formation," i.e., an invention of language. Anthropological reductionism has not only served as the premier belief system of Western scholars since the Enlightenment, it has also spawned the philosophical preoccupation with language and its codification into precise structures of meaning.

The tacit aim of this linguistic formalism has been to give knowledge an unshakable foundation in an age when one can no longer harken to ancient authorities, sacred scripture, or even what Kant and the eighteenth century understood as the "light of nature" and the universal power of reason. The older philosophies which made self-confident statements *de re* ("about things") gradually gave way to an indecisive and pathologically self-scrutinizing method of thought, which could only carry on a discussion *de dicto* ("concerning what is said"). Within language itself the followers of Russell and Wittgenstein were persuaded they would find the hitherto elusive philosopher's stone of "scientific certitude," whereby leaden ambiguity might be alchemized into gilt objectivity. Linguistic formalism and anthropological reductionism are different facets of the modernist conceit that man may "construct" his own world with the materials of introspection and rational analysis, then live comfortably within it. The exposure of this fraud has precipitated at last a fateful countermovement—that of *de-construction.* The movement of deconstruction has set about to show that the cathedral of modern intellect is but a mirage in cloud-cuckooland. Neither language nor human self-awareness conceals any thread of reference to things as they are. Hence, Derrida tells us, philosophers should not be so pretentious as to maintain they are writing "about" anything. Philosophy itself, according to Rorty, must be seen strictly as writing, rather than as any sort of "reflection" of the order of nature.[2] The same would hold for the claims of theology, perhaps with an even more gripping urgency.

II

Derrida's project of deconstruction has its genesis in the critique of metaphysical thinking launched by Nietzsche and worked out more intricately by Heidegger. The trumpet was sounded by Nietzsche in his *Twilight of the Idols.*

> The "true" world—an idea which is no longer good for anything, not even obligating—an idea which has become useless and superfluous—*consequently,* a refuted idea: let us abolish it![3]

Certain twentieth-century schools of philosophy have complied with Nietzsche's call for the transcendence of all naive realism in metaphysics and epistemology. Pragmatism and linguistic functionalism, which assess truth-claims à la Wittgenstein in terms of their "grammar" or "use in language," are the familiar products of such an assault on metaphysics. Yet these philosophical schools surreptitiously adopted their own peculiar "metaphysical" stance, inasmuch as they came to construe function in the same light as substance, utility as a substitute for validity, convention as a substitute for cogency. With the modernist revolt against the classical doctrine of correspondence between concepts and objects, words and things, along with its denial of the significance at any level of what Kant termed "noumena" or "things-in-themselves," there arose a new secular superstition—the belief that some sort of cognitive finality could be accorded to the phenomenal configurations of experience—to the historically relative forms of language, thought, and behavior themselves. Hence, both philosophers and theologians become immersed in intercultural comparisons and social linguistics.

Yet this insurrection against what Kant earlier denoted as metaphysical "dogmatism," or what commentators in the 1960s began to label by consensus as "ideology," could find no tablets on which the new Torah of truth might be graven. For, once the "true world" has been negated, "what world," Nietzsche asks, "has remained? The apparent one perhaps? But no! *With the true world we have also abolished the apparent one.*"[4] Deconstruction acknowledges that it is impossible to derive either a metaphyics or a method from what Foucault refers to as the modern "analytic of finitude." Thinking can no more be moored in its own constructs, or philosophy in semantics, than science is capable of proceeding simply from the philosophy of science. Just as nineteenth-century writers first saw through the masks of philosophical objectivity, so the movement of deconstruction challenges our contemporary "subjectism" (Heidegger's phrase), the massive illusion of self-reference.

For instance, when philosophy after Kant delimited the objects of cognition within the bounds of subjective preconceptions, it took refuge in the investigation of the conditions and structures of "consciousness," which encompassed not only phenomenology, but also humanistic Marxism. But the very notion of consciousness, as Nietzsche himself saw, is a feint and a deception. Nietzsche observes that consciousness is "really only a net of communication between human beings," a web of "signs." For "the world of which we can become conscious is only a surface- and sign-world."[5] The same theme has been embroidered in this century by linguistic philosophy, behaviorism, and semiotic theorists. The meaning of a word or a sentence is construed as its location in a cluster of significations; the "object" to which an expression "refers" is simply another set of sign-relations; the act of consciousness is the event of interpretation or mediation between these sets. Deconstruction incorporates within itself this fairly well-known critique of more traditional models of thought and linguistic meaning. Yet at the same time it denies *tout d'un coup* that the genesis and elaboration of signs within what philosophers casually delineate as the sphere of "discourse" coinheres with anything that might be straightaway conceived as reality. There has been the easy temptation among modernists to reify their own critical or metacritical perspectives, to assume that relativizing the contents of consciousness is sufficient to confer upon them a kind of factuality. For example, just because the Trobriander Islanders "see the world" differently than we do does not necessarily entail that either we or they see the world *at all*. Wittgenstein was correct when he contended that the limits of language are the limits of one's world, but that is not to say that language *is* the world.

Modernist thinking, which has traded for classical realism its own spurious metaphysics of self-reference, remains yoked to the fantasy of what Derrida dubs "the transcendental signified." The "transcendental signified" is that convergent object of reference to which all signs, or signifying elements, are somehow directed, even if this *ens realissimum* ("most real being"), as the medieval schoolmen named it, is nothing more than the prevailing pattern or "syntax" of verbal signification. The semantic notion of the transcendental signified, according to Derrida, is but the ghost of the Graeco-Christian God, a similacrum for the "Supreme Being."[6] It is based on the authoritarian sentiment of an eternal and immutable logos permeating the universe. Both the "divine word" (the agenda of theology) and "human speech" (the subject matter of anthropology) are born of what Derrida denotes as Western man's endemic "logocentrism." In place of all versions of the illusory transcendental signified, or what he elsewhere terms merely "presence" or the "tutelary meaning," Derrida proffers the unlimited "play" of signification itself. The spectrum of signification is open at both ends; at no point in the sign-process can we say that the "meaning" of a sentence or of a text, has been secured. Every moment of discourse qualifies and transforms what preceded it. "Reference" is never finalized, whether by intuition or by analysis. For the *referent* of a word, i.e., that which is signified by a token of language, consists primarily in an intransitive jump from sign to sign. As Derrida declares, the referent "functions only by giving rise to an *interpretant* that itself becomes a sign and so on to infinity. The self-identity of the signified conceals itself unceasingly and is always on the move."[7] Meaning is not what is signified, nor is it a relation between signifiers (linguistic functionalism), but is the endless *displacement* of one sign by its successor. Derrida proclaims boldly: "From the moment that there is meaning there are nothing but signs."[8]

Derrida underscores this rather radical account of language and meaning by enlarging upon three of his central concepts—"difference," "spacing," and "supplement." The notion of "difference" (*difference*) is perhaps the pivot of Derrida's global strategy of exposition. Derrida indicates that we generate new meanings not by addition, but by differentiation, dislocation, or distortion. Derrida takes as his paradigm case the French word *difference.* By a deliberate, yet simple misspelling (i.e., changing the vowel), Derrida fabricates his own technical neologism *difference,* which serves as philosophical shorthand for the movement of deconstruction. The "meaning" of *difference* emerges neither from the act of reference nor from the evaluation of semantic context, as is the case in linguistic functionalism. Instead it is an episodic figment, a violation of French orthography. But this violation is at the same time "institutionalized" and incised as the new word's "signification," although the new expression does not "point" to anything other than the lesion in spelling. A similar transfiguration takes place in the dispatch of tropes and metaphors. The metaphor literally "bends" the old meaning of the terms employed so as to create a new sense and usage. It is the bending and distension, however, which guarantees the phrase's metaphoric power. As regards deconstruction, therefore, meaning can be taken as differential in character. Yet it is not appropriate to say "the meaning as difference" of a locution, a metaphor, or a statement is tantamount to a tertium quid, an interpretant, or explanatory concept, that stands apart from the two terms differentiated. Meaning is the *moment of difference,* the divorce of familiar and alien connotations, the disengagement between the formal lexicon and language as an untrammeled, creative force. Meaning ensues when the alleged alterity or "otherness" which common sense tells us constitutes the realm for which all linguistic custom and innovation somehow "stands" (as in Nietzsche's "true world") is obliterated. This alterity, or what Derrida calls "presence," is revealed to be an *absence* by the grammatical or lexical infraction.

Thus, deconstruction represents a radical prospect for semantics and hermeneutics (the science of interpretation) whereby meaning in the formal sense is disclosed as *no-thingness.* Meaning is pure movement, the overflowing self-effacement of language. In this connection we must also adjudge meaning as the leaving of "traces," as Derrida calls it. A trace is "evidence" of something that paradoxically is not present at hand, but conspicuous through its absence. The trace is deposited by the movement of *differance.* Just as frequently we feel we "know" fully a man only after he has died and is no longer a tangible actuality, or we espy the "track" of a subatomic particle in a cloud chamber once it has vanished for all eternity, so we apprehend the meaning of an expression after it has been articulated and sundered from its unreflective immanence. Shall we say "died" to the letter? Indeed, death or nihilation is what "lies behind" the strands of linguistic meaning. Derrida writes somewhat cryptically: "Death, which is neither a present to come nor a present past, shapes the interior of speech, as its trace, its reserve, its interior and exterior differance."[9] No-thingness is the eschatological limit of all language, just as death comprises the teleology of all life. Deconstruction and the fecundity of meaning realized from the process of difference is ingredient in and absolutely vital to the "living" logos. For that reason we may claim that deconstruction is the opposite of stylistic libertinism and the self-conscious nihilism of so many earlier "metaphysical" attempts (e.g., Jean-Paul Sartre) to demonstrate that discourse and the phenomenality of the world, including our own self-awareness, are but ripples in the void, shudders across a sea of emptiness. Deconstruction is the internal and self-propelled dismantling (as well as the equable reshaping) of the structures of understanding and meaning like the chick that shatters the egg, or the moth that bursts the chrysalis. In Derrida's words,

> . . . the movements of deconstruction do not destroy structures from the outside. They are possible and effective, nor can they take accurate aim, except by inhabiting those structures. Inhabiting them *in a certain way,* because one always inhabits, and all the more when one does not suspect it. Operating necessarily from the inside, borrowing all the strategic and economic resources of subversion from the old structure, borrowing them structurally, that is to say without being able to isolate their elements and atoms, the enterprise of deconstruction always in a certain way falls prey to its own work.[10]

Differance, or difference, is the continuous production of significance through displacement. For if language genuinely did consist in the game of referring or de-signating, there could be no linguistic enterprise, no invention, no release from the Babylonian captivity of formal logic and exegetical rigor.

The ruse of reference, Derrida suggests, is manufactured out of the primordial human longing for a return to origins, for a retreat from history back to paradise. The path of consciousness, thought, and linguistic development, which demarcates man's historical existence, is always rectilinear. However, the nostalgic lure of preconsciousness—the seduction of innocence—is inscribed in *circular* characters. Language and interpretation, like the movement of reflection, are deflected toward their own absent beginnings. They are etched within the legend of presence. And since Western philosophy is a Golem of Western linguistic dispositions, it is only to be expected that the former would be bedazzled, albeit with dash and finesse, by the legend. The search for the Rosetta stone of reference in modern linguistics and semiotics is a chapter in what Derrida regards as the "idealistic" bewitchment of thought, the impulse to leap into the magic circle of a self-enfolding discourse and dance the hypnotic rondo of "verification" and "certitude." Such a desire Derrida faults as "stupefying" and "scandalous"; it is the motive behind "the entirety of a philosophy founded on the illusory reappropriation of alterity in the different forms of idealism.[11] Alterity or "otherness" must remain *totaliter aliter* ("wholly other"); furthermore, such alterity must come to light when the razor-straight vector of all language and thinking is confirmed and the ancient wraith of circularity disperses into the night. Every quantum of discourse cancels itself in the moment of "expression." It does not express anything except a "space" between itself and what was said before it. The world line of evolving logos, therefore, is a fractured one.

Deconstruction is the "deconstitution" of idealism. But this deconstitution proceeds according to the law of "spacing" (*espacement*). Precisely speaking, "spacing is the impossibility for an identity to be closed on itself, on the inside of its proper interiority, or on its coincidence with itself. The irreducibility of spacing is the irreducibility of the other."[12] Spacing disallows any logical possibility of a Hegelian *Aufhebung,* a transcendental synthesis of polarities. For polarities (or differences) in discourse and cognition lend impetus to the very movement of deconstructive meaning. "Negated presence," not the "negation of the negation," the spurious ideality of what Hegel in his circular idiom denotes as "the return of the concept unto itself," is the *vis viva,* the "vital force," of all language. "Spacing" is the indication of the trace, the opening into the bountiful and meaning-laden void amid the interstices of grammar. A father's anger is accented in his deliberate silence; Sherlock Holmes solves the murder by noting the dog who *didn't* bark. Consummation is an evacuation; *noesis* ("thinking") is *kenosis* ("emptying"). Derrida states that "*spacing* designates *nothing,* nothing that is, no presence at a distance; it is the index of an irreducible exterior, and at the same time of a *movement.*[13]

The movement of spacing, like the event of deconstruction, is the revelation of all substance as emptiness. But spacing and deconstruction are not mysterious fibers of dissolution knitted into the linguistic batik; they are not some intractable death instinct within the organism of meaning. Deconstruction itself is a function of the self-movement of language from "inside" to "outside," from spirit to letter, from code to message, from implication to explication, from intention to communication, from speech to *writing*. Indeed, the facticity of writing is what not only makes deconstruction possible, but confirms it as the sturdy destiny of the seemingly "immortal" logos. In writing, language attains its essential materiality, its embodiment, and henceforth its identity. The fugitive indication of the *phonē*, or vocalized utterance, is transmuted into the enduring representation that we recognize as the "written word," as the grapheme. Only this graphic eternalization of speech as what can properly from a philosophical standpoint be termed "discourse" allows for reflection on the phenomenon of *language* as well as the investigation of "meaning." For a term can only "mean" something, let alone "refer" or denote, once it is capable of semantic reduplication—that is, representation through repetition. And the possibility of repetition springs from the device of *depiction*. The first hieroglyph or ideogram was the occasion for the thought that a language act *bespeaks* something other than itself, or the "thing" designated. Writing introduced into man's circuit of self-knowledge the intuition of a new vector in the field of verbal force. Beside the unfathomable monad of signification there sprung into consciousness the supposition of the independent *signifier*. Before the institution of writing, perhaps the modern idea of the separation between language and reality, which we now take for granted, was inconceivable. For the *phonē* had nothing against which to calibrate and reprogram itself. In fact, philologists tell us that the further back we probe into the archives of a linguistic tradition the more it becomes plain the "meaning" of a word is the same as a concrete occurrence (e.g., the fact, with which most students of biblical theology are acquainted, that the Hebrew *dabar* can be translated as both "word" and "event").

The replacement of the oracle by the inscription led to the sense of a permanent presence for all dicta or sayings. This permanent presence became the fiction of the *signified*. The signified, in turn, generated the presumption of the "idea" of the thing, which was alleged to be somehow coordinate with its linguistic counterpart. Philosophy and metaphysics were born when the "ideas" began to inhabit a plane of their own. Benjamin Whorff, the great anthropologist and linguist, was right when he hypothesized that all thought systems and world pictures are projections of language. But he overlooked the fundamental condition of linguistic projection—the act of writing down. The idea is impossible without the representation; the analysis of reference hinges inextricably on the concept of *grammar* (which derives from the Greek word "to write").

Plato, however, was wrong when at the end of the *Phaedrus* he argued that philosophy would be purer if it remained in the preliterary phase of Socratic dialogue, if the contemplation of the ideas were prior to the reading of texts. For the written text itself is what conjures the alterity of the word, the word that can be glimpsed in the looking glass of philosophy as the idea or universal "form" (*eidos*). Disciplined thought is begotten of language through the midwivery of writing. In that connection what Derrida terms *grammatology*—the science of writing—must supplant the encrusted routines of philosophy. If philosophy, and theology for that matter, is "about" anything, it is about things in their modes of representation. But the mode of representation is abstracted from the grammatological context. Thus both philosophy and theology through an inquiry into the forms of writing and their semantic peculiarities can uncover their own agenda and aim. But if the "subject matter" of an intellectual regimen such as theology is alloyed, and can be seen in some sense as consubstantial, with writing as an autonomous agency, then that about which the discipline "speaks" is language in its rude exteriority. And beneath this exteriority is buried the "secret" of all traditions of structured discourse—that they "signify nothing." In our day, for instance, philosophical reflection has been absorbed into the analysis of language. Theology since Barth has been consumed with the "therapeutic" task of clarifying its own logic and surveying its domains of discourse. Such a narcissism of method, nonetheless, is but a backhanded recognition of the point Derrida emphasizes. If theology, instead of examining the nature and attributes of God, or even exploring the meaning and discursive function of the holy name, becomes preoccupied in contrast with pondering the purpose for which it is "done," then it must come to understand itself *strictu sensu* as a meditation within discourse upon discourse. The divine word, the *sacra verba,* is truly made flesh; it reaches its kenotic consummation, its radical otherness, in a theology which is nought but a writing about theology. Of late one hears nervous gossip among theologians that no one reads them much anymore. For how can one read theology when its logos has been sublimated into writing. Reading implies that there is something more to be garnered from a text than the affectations of the text alone. In that regard it is elegantly plausible why we have arrived at the end of theology.

Theology, like writing, consists in what Derrida calls a "supplement." The idea of supplement is bound up with the notions of both addition and substitution. The supplement "carries on" from where the primary text left off. In that regard it is something "appended to" the initial body of discourse. But this appendage is a supplement, not a *complement,* to what remains anterior to it. It is qualitatively different, and its *difference* resides in its performance whereby the text is consistently altered. It is cognate, but not *conjoint,* with what it supplements. Derrida uses the deliberately shocking example of masturbation to exemplify his concept of the supplement. Masturbation is prima facie a type of genital sexuality; the same "act" as in ordinary intercourse transpires. Yet masturbation is a differential modification of both the experience and goal of the sex act. It satisfies no "objective" other than the pleasure stimulus, the "release" of tension. It discloses the vacuity of the "thing" supplemented. "It is the strange essence of the supplement not to have essentiality . . . the supplement is neither a presence nor an absence. No ontology can think its operation."[14] No ontology is capable of thinking the supplement, because the latter does not signify anything beyond itself. According to Derrida, all metaphysical speculation—the twenty-five-hundred-year search inaugurated by Aristotle for the *ens qua ens,* "being as Being"—is but a fumbling after shadows. For the concept of Being represents the ultimate projection of grammar, the *Doppelgänger* or dark double of all logical predication, the phantom signature of what Derrida calls "the supplement of the copula." Metaphysics is a supplement, a fractious substitution, for naive discourse "about things," which in turn is a supplement for the bare utterance. The thought of Being or "truth" is tantamount to an "intrusion within language's closure upon itself."[15]

Furthermore, this closure is what renders language as *dis-course* (i.e., "a flowing away from") a dependent variable of writing. For Derrida, there is no *archē* or semantic origin for what is said in discourse. Nor is there any end or completion, a metamorphosis of connotation into direct reference. The supplement is the interminable motion of meaning, which is equivalent to the dynamics of writing and rewriting. Writing, however, is more than the "putting words on paper." It is the ongoing enfleshment and displacement—shall we say the "crucifixion"?—of the eternal "Word" by its diffusion within and through time. "Writing" is a *wrenching;* it activates what Derrida characterizes as "the violence of the letter." The violence is contained in the very history of writing. The ancient archetypes, the immutable patterns of thought and expression, are tortured and shattered. "Writing" comes from the Indo-Aryan root *war,* which means "to cut" or "tear" (as in the German *reissen*). The modern sensibility, which has been responsible for the overthrow of the medieval view of the cosmos as cyclical and hierarchical, had its inception in the sixteenth century; it was the century of Luther and the printing press, wherein was launched both a prolix "Protestant" theology and the expansion of academic discourse into all extremities of the "secular" realm. The sixteenth and seventeenth centuries were exceptionally violent ones, inasmuch as they marked the birth of modern "writing." Philosophy moved out of the university and monastery; the epic became the novel.

III

If the sixteenth century was the age in which "writing" was divulged as the hitherto concealed nature of logos, it was also the historical moment, if we follow the analysis of Michel Foucault, when "man" was invented, not as a corporeal creature, but as a "formation" of discourse. Anthropology, according to Foucault, would be impossible without this grammatical projection made possible by writing, by the solidification of the very "subject" of autonomous discourse. The sixteenth century, which gave free commission to writing, also brought into existence "the author." Foucault maintains that the author is a product of the Reformation; he is the "authority" who adjudicates the function and authenticity of texts. Prior to the decline of clerical prerogative, along with the impugning of the homogeneous sanctity of what the church without qualification claimed as *traditio,* in the sixteenth century the author was subordinate to the text, which in turn was taken as an elaboration or true reflection of the divine mind. Hermeneutics mirrored the dogmas of metaphysics. Even though monks scribbled away the centuries in their cloisters, writing had not yet emerged as the root metaphor for meaning. Medieval theology was steeped in oral conversation; linguistic theory was caught up with a semantics of the voice. *Deus dixit* ("God says") served as the supreme criterion of "authorial" validation. Once the Reformers had exposed this particular imprimatur, however, as an excuse for papal swagger and replaced it with the principle of *sola Scriptura* ("by Scripture alone"), which was in effect to exchange the hierophany of speech for the luminosity of the "Book," then it became necessary to conjure up the "author" upon whom any promiscuous deviations of "interpretation" could be blamed. According to Foucault, the author was the one who could be "punished" for any distortion of the proper text. Given the boundless and potentially chaotic variations of meaning that could be spawned from the act of writing, the author was devised as the agency of constraint. Foucault writes:

> The author allows a limitation of the cancerous and dangerous proliferation of significations within a world where one is thrifty not only with one's resources and riches, but also with one's discourses and their significations. The author is the principle of thrift in the proliferation of meaning. As a result, we must entirely reverse the traditional idea of the author. We are accustomed . . . to saying that the author is the genial creator of a work in which he deposits, with infinite wealth and generosity, an inexhaustible world of significations. We are used to thinking that the author is so different from all other men, and so transcendent with regard to all languages that, as soon as he speaks, meaning begins to proliferate, to proliferate indefinitely. The truth is quite the contrary . . . the author does not precede the works, he is a certain functional principle by which . . . one limits, excludes, and chooses . . . by which one impedes the free circulation, the free manipulation, the free composition, decomposition, and recomposition of fiction.[16]

The author, however, turned out to be something more monumental than the cachet for literary and intellectual certification. The author became the chrysalis for a whole new conception, a style of reflection that was strange, if not utterly foreign to the classical and medieval *auctoritas,* or ancient outlook. Authorship supplanted "authority," sacred doctrine gave place to the testament of individual conscience in the arbitration of philosophical disputes and the appropriation of new thoughts. With the development of authorship both "man" and the active, autonomous linguistic "signifier" came into existence. Moreover, the constitution of the one coincided with the fabrication of the other. Man as author, as the *subject* of discourse, became a synonym for the "transcendental signified" of Derrida. Only man possessed, as the Romantics would finally convert into a formal proposition in the early nineteenth century, the aptitude for language. But this exclusive "human" talent could only be registered and dissected in tandem with the classification of its subject. Anthropology, philology, and cultural linguistics were all constructed out of the same modern discursive "set," as Foucault calls it. "Man" himself could not be thrown into symbolic relief until *discourse* itself was disentangled from the web of natural relations. When language was cut loose in the early modern period from where it has been situated in Renaissance thinking—as part of the "prose of the world," the Book of Nature—man as the primal self-referent of all language rose to prominence as an appropriate theme for endless inquiry.

Before this modern "transvaluation" of ancient values the notion of man as the linguistic animal, Foucault maintains, was embedded in a skein of overlapping representations. Representation itself was not taken as skill of man, or as an effect of language, sui generis as it came to be understood in the twentieth century. At the same time, the anthropological profile of man uniquely as self-conscious, i.e., as capable of *representing himself,* would have jarred with the premier theological idea of the "soul" as the *speculum mundi,* the "mirror" of the universe and of the Creator. Representation, in the medieval and Renaissance estimate of things, belonged to the cosmic grid of "resemblances." Language was simply a particular vehicle of resemblance, as a transitional plane in the palpable "network of signs that crosses the world from one end to another." Words were not disjoined from entities in the same way as authority and "truth" were not functionally differentiated, as they now are.

In the epoch that preceded the age of anthropology and semiology, Foucault asserts,

> . . . there is no difference between marks and words in the sense that there is between observation and accepted authority, or between verifiable fact and tradition. The process is everywhere the same: that of the sign and its likeness, and this is why nature and the word can intertwine with one another to infinity, forming, for those who can read it, one vast single text.[17]

The text or the "Book" is a compendium not of grammatical operators, signifiers, and logical connectives, as we find in contemporary accounts of how language "means" as it does, but of *things* in their affinities and similitudes with one another. Meaning is correspondence, not as a one-to-one factor, but as a lattice of reciprocal and reversible implications between creatures who in their very singularity give hint of the glory of their universal Maker. "The great metaphor of the book that one opens, that one pores over and reads in order to know nature, is merely the reverse and visible side of another transference, and a much deeper one, which forces language to reside in the world, among the plants, the herbs, the stones, and the animals."[18]

Prior to the sixteenth century, Foucault suggests, the logos was intimately braided with the whole of reality, inasmuch as it was perceived as the divine template of visible creation, the mystic fountainhead of matter and spirit alike. The rupture of language from nature which later took place, then, signaled the exile of logos, the transformation of the medieval system of resemblances and likenesses into a *game* of signs and disincarnate representations. Man himself became a sign, a cipher that roused the need for a new "science" of anthropology. The modern *de-sign* of man was conceived when language and thinking could no longer be accepted as a moment in "mirroring" or "speculative" activity of the infinite intelligence; they were now regarded as separate artifacts, as representations or images not of their transcendent origin, but of their immanent semblances. The mirror began to mirror itself; and behind it philosophy surmised an empty backdrop. The glow in the mirror was no longer the *lumen naturale,* the "light of nature," but the shimmer of "human reason," the artificial glint of *Aufklärung,* or Enlightenment. Language and thought became frost wisps in the windowpane of *self-reflection.* In his fireside musings Descartes found it easier to doubt God than to doubt the ego, the subject of thought, the *author* of language. His meditations compelled him for the sake of metaphysical consistency to hypostatize the *I* of the "I think" as a *res cogitans,* a thinking "thing." Over the next three hundred years the thinking thing was able to think all resemblances first as conventions, then as mirages. Descartes was the father of French philosophy; he was also the ancestral demon of deconstruction.

Descartes, we may infer from Foucault, was the first anthropologist to the extent that he seized, mastered, and impressed logos into a strenuous regimen of self-disclosure. Descartes gave man, the subject, an ontological warrant for his nascent obsession with himself. But this Cartesian liberation of language from what the seventeenth-century philosophers considered its lengthy career of theological tutelage and its subsequent redeployment toward the "independent" subject matters of man and nature was not without its cost. For the magic ring of self-reference, once snatched by a thieving Hermes from the caverns of consciousness, proved to be something of a danger in the hands of acolytes. As Goya would later exclaim, "the dream of reason breeds monsters."

And what was the next of these monstrosities? Back of the empty mirror of Cartesian reflection could be described the demon of madness. As Foucault observes, madness has been the recurring nightmare of our modern "anthropological sleep." Madness is the remainder, the offscouring, the detritus of modern culture's attempt to "confine" truth and existence within the preserve of human "needs" and self-awareness. The modern history of asylums in which the madman was "put away" from society, cordoned, shut up, and kept out of the public gaze, certifies this approach to insanity. Just as modern epistemology with a binary rigidity divided experience into veracity (whatever was "clear and distinct" in the Cartesian sense) and error (what was ambiguous and not foursquare "verifiable"), so

> . . . confinement merely manifested what madness, in its essence was: a manifestation of non-being; and by providing this manifestation, confinement thereby suppressed it, since it restored it to its truth as nothingness. Confinement is the practice which corresponds most exactly to madness experienced as unreason, that is, as the empty negativity of reason; by confinement, madness is acknowledged to be nothing.[19]

Madness and nothingness all along have been the chained Titans in the dungeon of a once cocksure modernity. Modern civilization has sought both to enlarge the kingdom of reason and to subjugate madness in the sovereign name of *humanitas*. This campaign, by Foucault's analysis, contrasts decisively with the awe and reverence in which the demented man of the Middle Ages was held. He was considered an emissary from "the other world"; his lunacy, as in Plato's time, was viewed as charisma, an infusion of divine energy, a mark not of Cain but of Enoch. The medieval madman did not appear "sick" or "misfortunate"; he was merely *unapproachable.* He was the sacred sojourner in society rather than its shame. The madman's presence sufficed as a spiritual ligament between the different "worlds" that reflected each other; respect for him was vital to the preservation of the cosmic ecology. When modern penitential theory, and later psychiatry, undertook to confine and afterwards to "cure" him, they also succeeded in warping the divine inkling behind his countenance. The plenitude of divine presence was reassessed as the negativity of *unreason;* saintliness became *insanity;* light was made darkness.

Whereas the Middle Ages and the Renaissance had symbolized otherness as the unfathomable mystery of the God who reigned above and beyond the empirical order, in the modern era the divine alterity was imagined anew as the darkness "within," a parlous and unruly "enthusiasm," the temptation to become ensnared in dreams, superstitions, and fantasies. Foucault remarks that

> . . . the Cartesian formula of doubt is certainly the great exorcism of madness. Descartes closes his eyes and plugs up his ears the better to see the true brightness of essential daylight; thus he is secured against the dazzlement of the madman who, opening his eyes, sees only night, and not seeing at all, believes he sees when he imagines.[20]

The modern myth of self-reference could only be sustained by madness; psychiatrists became modern society's wizards and witch doctors, rational discourse and the "reality principle" their apotropaic wands. Just as the shadowy Furies of Aeschylean tragedy were, in essence, the vengeful phantoms of an older and repressed goddess worship, so the specter of madness in the modern setting is the underside of a cowed religiosity. Jung, at least, understood that. From the outset madness has been the unspoken complication of that course of thought which has heeded Feuerbach's appeal for theology to become anthropology, or it might be better to say of those who have genuinely followed through on the dictum. It is no surprise that the death of God is announced by Nietzsche's madman, expostulating that "all of us are his murderers." Nietzsche's madman, who intrudes into the sunny marketplace of modernist anthropocentrism, is in truth *everyman.* For the madmen, who are at the same time the murderers of God, have incurred their affliction as compensation for their attempt not to storm but to fence off and subdivide heaven.

Barely do we read Nietzsche's parable as collective self-confession; nor do we glimpse the madman as a kind of post-Enlightenment, blinded Oedipus who has finally seen clearly the meaning of his effort to play God, a decadent hypersensibility or vacuous narcissism which is the spur to incest in the first place. Deconstruction can be taken as the intellectual equivalent of the madman's casting down of his lantern.

Nevertheless, Foucault's "anthropological sleep" constitutes a failure to detect an even more faint, yet far and away more critical tempo within the unfolding rhythm of historical consciousness. We are alluding, of course, to the change in our view of the divine from alterity to immediacy, from transcendence to immanence, from occultation to what Tom Altizer has dubbed "total presence." The metaphor, if not the "sacrament," for this event is the regicide performed during the English and French revolutions, which may be counted as the historical bridge between modern culture and its antecedent forms. The execution of the monarch was the cutting off of the *caput sanctum,* the "sacred head," of Christendom or God's visible empire. With the killing of the king there was no longer any authoritative representative of heaven in the earthly domain. The event can be taken as the terrestrial analogue to the murder of God. The regicide sealed the destiny of the revolution, the sacrifice of absolutism to the emboldened canaille. But this revolt at the same time ushered in the anthropological eon. Divine right passed over into the "rights of man." Furthermore, the assertion of human "rights" was coincident with the redistribution of *power.* Before the dawn of modern democratic society, power was both local and concentrated in the person of the sovereign. The sovereign's power was upheld through his majesty, singularity, and distance from those over whom he wielded his scepter. But the perpetration of regicide corresponded to the *kenosis* and dissipation of this power throughout the newly enfranchised and embryonically self-conscious masses. From the political side, the spectacle of the gallows in the market square was the modern Calvary. Regicide signified the destruction of the great tutelary icon, the effacement of the last societal vessel of transcendence. Future historians of the decline and fall of the Western world will probably recognize, if they happen to be clever, that the execution of the king was contemporary with the extinction of the holy man or saint. The deconstruction of the "transcendental signified" shares a deep structure with the "humanistic" and egalitarian ethos that has prevailed since the first Bastille day.

The modern economy of power, which has its center of gravity at the base of the sociopolitical pyramid, rather than in the tip, is not only democratic, but thoroughly *material* in its embodiments. Regicide, or decapitation, meant that the ganglion of power was transferred from the head to the torso, to the broad "body politic." Hence, we might say that "democracy" is an inexact construction so far as it can be relied upon to impart the more profound currents of modernist ideology. Possibly a better word would be *somacracy*—the rule of the "body." Somacracy camouflaged as the "democratic" principle has resulted in an exchange of the articles of transcendence. The arrow of eros was reversed; the soul no longer thirsted for other-worldly beatitude, but for the *jouissance* of what Christianity had derogated as the "flesh." As Foucault notes, sexuality has become the obsession of the modern mind for good reason: it is the surrogate of transcendence for a civilization that has severed itself at the neck. And, just as sexuality, in contraposition to the cerebral functions of will and judgment, spreads out over the entire *soma,* the multiple gradients of the physical nervous system, so "power" in the modern body politic is decentralized, polyvalent, and insidiously resilient. The older monarchial metaphors of repression and rebellion, which continue to crop up in the argot of sexual libertinism, are irrelevant to the modern situation. The premodern schematism of power was imagined in accordance with the ascendance of the head over the greater corpus; power implied *co-ercion,* singular force, *volition*. The "will of God" and the fiat of royalty matched the psycho-physical dualism of decadent antiquity and medieval piety. On the other hand, the modern *incorporation* of power, its transmission from spirit to libido, has led to an inversion of the symbols of power. Power as coercion is negative and tyrannical; power as *somatic satisfaction* is positive and thereby more entrenched. Modern power "holds good," Foucault contends, because it does not "weigh on us as a force that says no"; instead, it "induces pleasure." "It needs to be considered as a productive network which runs through the whole social body, much more than as a negative instance whose function is repression."[21] If "power is strong this is because . . . it produces effects at the level of desire—and also at the level of knowledge."[22] These immanent "micro-relations" of power are what bind together modern society—its bureaucratic stanchions, stupefied laborers, mindless revelers—and the effect is like that of a steel mesh. If the mesh is tugged or stretched in one direction, it is thereby made taut in a neighboring region, creating a rigid tension, so that when the distorting force is spent, the original configuration returns.

Moreover, in the same way that somacracy has a structure, so it has a language of legitimation, a discourse. Foucault realizes that power and discourse are covalent with each other. "Discourse transmits and produces power; it reinforces it."[23] The "multiplicity of discursive elements" compose the "strategies" of power, and power logistics are dependent on discourse—of propaganda. Humanism is not only the "religion" of secular modernity, but its core formation of power, knowledge, and language. Anthropology is doubtlessly theology in this sense—it has not only its scholars but its ecclesia and inquisition. The discursive center of modern thought is actually polycentric; it represents the multitude of discourses, politely termed "pluralism," that has matured in this century as the idée fixe of the so-called "human sciences." Such a pluralism is vaunted as the guarantee of liberty, if not "liberation." It is positioned in defiance of "power," which is linked conceptually with repression.

But the converse is actually the case. The discourse of pluralism masks an apologetics of passivity. And this passivity exhibits itself as a criticism that is no longer critical, as an instinctual carnival that is in brute fact an amnesia, an eclipse of knowledge. For knowledge requires a sense of the universal more than a shuffling of particulars. The genital piety of the "theologians of the body," the most notorious of whom is naturally Norman O. Brown, is nurtured on the pluralist opiate that sustains the anthropological sleep.

In the anthropological sleep all sorts of disturbed and fleeting dream signatures creep about, wherein the modern analytic of finitude becomes "the analytic of everything that can, in general, be presented to man's experience."[24] To be sure, discourse turns in upon itself in an overrefinement of its hues and nuances; knowledge becomes proportionately more discriminated, more self-referential, and more *inconsequential.* Foucault concludes his *Order of Things* with an apocalyptic cymbal clash:

> And precisely when this language (of finitude and modernity) emerges in all its nudity, yet at the same time eludes all signification as if it were a vast and empty despotic system, when Desire reigns in the wild state, as if the rigor of its rule had leveled all opposition, when Death dominates every psychological function and stands above it as its unique and devastating norm—then we recognize madness in its present form, madness as it is posited in the modern experience, as its truth and its alterity . . . it no longer observes the wandering of a straying reason; it sees welling up that which is, perilously, nearest to us—as if, suddenly, the very hollowness of our existence is outlined in relief; *the finitude upon the basis of which were, are, and think, and know, is suddenly there before us.*[25]

Deconstruction is the immolation of the transcendental signified; but does it quench itself in the infinite,

Cimmerian sea of madness, in which we are all chattel of Poseidon? Foucault steps back from the brink where Derrida exhorts us to plunge.

IV

Again, we must underscore our leading thesis: deconstruction is the death of God put into writing. In that respect the movement of deconstruction *within* theology rounds out the enigmatic anticipation of the end-times. But it is theology's "ending" not in glory, but forsakenness. The *theologia crucis,* the "theology of the cross," is at last translated from a style of intellectual voyeurism into an evident ordeal: it becomes the *crux theologiae.* Before the arrival of the moment of deconstruction, theology has been able to speak with a leonine pride of salutary signifiers concerning the meaning of the word *God.* Yet it has been unable, or unwilling, to utter the consummatory cry of its own crucified Lord—*Tetelestai!* "It is finished." Theology still holds on to its erstwhile "constructive" task; it is paralyzed and indisposed to give up the ghost. Nietzsche's parable poses as a teasing riddle rather than as the handwriting on the wall. But if God dies, so must theology. A "death of God theology" is, and always was, an oxymoron, a tasteless jape, a *tour de farce.* The revelation of the farce is writing; and theology must write itself into the grave.

Deconstruction within theology writes the epitaph for the dead God. But the death of God is not necessarily a cause for celebration. Theologians who might appropriate Nietzsche's great "myth" for their own vanity or personal aggrandizement are like children who have discovered some black and treacherous abracadabra. The madman is our reminder of the "price" of deconstruction to be paid by those who remain dilettantes, polished peacocks, or glib wordsmiths. Even Nietzsche himself, his mind still thunderstruck by the vision of Overman, was powerless to evade the fate of his own literary messenger. Deconstruc-

tion is the *descensus in infernus,* the venture into the underworld of limitless writing, the dismembering of all names
and concepts, the dance of Dionysus. When Nietzsche in
his terminal insanity signed his correspondence "Dionysus
or the Crucified," he was not calling attention to a disjunction, but to a hidden identity. Dionysus, like the Crucified
One, shatters all regimen, providence, and formality;
Dionysus is the dancer. And as James Hillman reminds us:

> There is a dance in death. Hades and Dionysus are the
> same.[26]

Deconstruction is the dance of death upon the tomb of
God; it is the tarantella whose footfalls evoke the archaism
of the Great Mother, who takes back with the solemnity of
the Pietà her wounded, divine son.

Deconstruction, therefore, can be seen as a kind of
Bacchic fascination with the metaphysics of decomposition
and death, with the murky undercurrent of modern
discourse; in this respect it serves as a simile for the return
of the repressed feminine in a predominantly patriarchal
academy. How are we otherwise to comprehend Derrida's
obsession with *la femme?* Indeed, Derrida self-consciously
compares woman to the movement of deconstruction.

> There is no essence of woman because woman separates, and
> separates herself off from herself. From the endless, bottom-
> less depths, she submerges all essentiality, all identity, all
> propriety, and every property. Blinded in such a way, philo-
> sophical discourse flounders, and is left to dash headlong to
> its ruin. There is no truth about woman, just because this
> abysmal separation from truth, this nontruth, is *the* "truth."
> Woman is one name for this nontruth of truth.[27]

Such rhetoric quashes any notion that the sentiment of
deconstruction is *feminist.* Feminism does not banish
woman to nothingness. On the contrary, we detect in
Derrida's idiom the cloying sensation of *fin de siécle*

nihilism. For Derrida, the deconstructionist "posture" is not so much that of the feminist, but of the womanizer, the dandy. For Derrida, writing is the *éperon,* ("spur"), the phallic signifier that has renounced all representative fidelity and turned promiscuous. It is "like the prow . . . of a sailing vessel, its *rostrum,* the projection of the ship which surges ahead to meet the sea's attack and cleave its hostile surface."[28] The dandy cajoles, seduces, drives and manipulates the "inessential" feminine style, the Muse or *mus-ic* behind what Julia Kristeva terms "heteronymy," or the "power of an open infinity," the unrelieved temporalization of logos, the reduction of meaning to rhythm, the disintegration of all representation into instinct and *desire.*[29]

In consequence, deconstruction is assuredly the disporting of Dionysus. Dionysus incites the unconscious and "savage" force of the chthonic feminine. As in Euripides' play, the *Bacchae,* he is the mischievous and unscrupulous adolescent who brandishes his "spur" as an invitation to chaos. He is the power of puerile instinct. He annoys, charms, and finally "deconstructs" the good bourgeois Pentheus, whose civility and morality are moribund and hence no match for the intoxicated women of the forest. But at the same time he is also "master" of Pentheus's mother, Agave, who at Dionysus's prodding kills her own son in an animal frenzy without a scintilla of awareness as to what she is doing. And in the end we find ourselves boggled by the scene, by the bathos of a gruesome tragedy. Dionysus is the same as the crucified, but a crucifixion without the Christian "hope" of the resurrection.

If Dionysus is the instigator, he is at the same time the spectator. And he is a spectator because he is the technician, not the participant, in the tragedy. In addition, he is a spectator on account of his *immortal* nature. Hence, the Titans may rip him asunder, but they cannot crucify him. Nietzsche, too, coveted the immortality of Dionysus. Even though he reveled in the murder of God, he could not divest himself of the longing for "life everlasting." His answer to finitude was the great "thought" of eternal recurrence. The myth of Dionysus, as appropriated in the postmodern era, battens on the horror of mortality. By the same token, deconstruction as a Dionysian dance of discourse constitutes a clandestine wish for immortality through writing. God dies, but *inscription* survives. The end of theology is palliated by the renovation of the art of theological writing, even writing *about* deconstruction. Although the dandy pontificates about the death wish, he himself is terrified of dying. He praises the collapse of all institutions and representations, of grammar together with structure, yet he yearns fervently to preserve his own pride of place as a prestigious interpreter of the *Götterdämmerung,* the great "twilight of the gods." Deconstruction can never be authentic if it rises to the status of a vogue within theology, for nothing is more reprehensible than making a cultus out of what ought to be the criticism of every cultus. A "theology of deconstruction" would be nothing more than a sophisticated perversion, a literary necrophilia.

Nonetheless, the pitfalls of any attempt to "domesticate" the movement of deconstruction—for instance, by elevating the host of writing—cannot be offset by the nostalgia of "reconstruction." Regardless of the previous caveats and cavils, we must confront the somber fact that the movement of deconstruction is inevitable and cannot be averted by revanchist maneuvers. Deconstruction is the flailing of the spades of God's gravediggers. To refuse the ceremony of burial, however, is a more culpable form of hubris than to take the shovel in hand. For the stench of "divine decomposition," as Nietzsche phrased it, is everywhere. The deconstruction of God, then, is comparable to the stern aunt at the Irish wake who, having abided long enough the innocent but fatuous comments, "Uncle Jules looks like he's still with us," finally blurts out, "Nonsense, the old stiff's cold as granite." The deconstruction of God coincides with the end of theology; but it also indicates the close of the Augustan era of anthropology and anthropological habits of thinking. For, as we have seen, *theos* and *anthropos* are both formations of discourse that epitomize the classical and postclassical periods respectively. They are the systole and diastole of historical consciousness. Truly the death of God is the demise of man, as some detractors two decades ago in that Indian summer of twentieth-century "humanism" wrung their hands and lamented. But the demise of man is only the toppling of the last icon of the great cycle. The myth of the God-man, promoted by the eighteenth-century *illuminati*, was replaced by the nineteenth-century saga of the man-god.

Yet no matter which term occupies the left of the hyphen, the same abstraction, the same semantic constellation mistaken for a determinate object of inquiry, remains. Deconstruction rubs out the hyphen, transmutes stiff nouns into supple verbs, converts the reified representations into fluid discourse. Deconstruction does not announce the death of God through writing in order to install a new fetishism, a kind of *anthropomancy,* the mumbo-jumbo of pronouncing the awesome name of "humanity." Neither does it elide the transcendental signified in order to provide a commercial bonanza for publishers, a sort of art nouveau that banks on caricature, a new sensation in an age jaded with sensations and conditioned to compulsively consume what is advertised as *difference,* even if it is totally misunderstood. The omega moment of deconstruction is when the *movement* of deconstruction deconstructs itself, when the book that in the modern age became a text, or the weave of resemblances that became a nest of signifiers, is at last transfigured into the uncrystallized expanse of luminosity and intelligence. Deconstruction is the eschatology of the twenty-five-hundred-year epoch of logos. It is the groaning and travail of the transformation of word as logos ("representation") into word as *rhema* ("flow"). It is Nietzsche's third metamorphosis of the spirit, the most arduous transposition, the passage from the lion's spurring to the child's innocence. It is neither exclusively the word made flesh, nor the flesh sublated in the word; it is . . .

NOTES

1. See Richard Rorty, *Philosophy and the Mirror of Nature* (Princeton: Princeton University Press, 1979).

2. See Richard Rorty, "Philosophy as a Kind of Writing: An Essay on Derrida," in *New Literary History* 10 (1978): 141–60.

3. Friedrich Nietzsche, "Twilight of the Idols," in Walter Kaufmann, ed., *The Portable Nietzsche* (New York: Viking Press, 1954).

4. "Twilight of the Idols," p. 486.

5. Friedrich Nietzsche, *The Gay Science*, trans. Walter Kaufmann (New York: Random House, 1974), p. 299.

6. Consider Derrida's remarks: ". . . the intelligible face of the sign remains turned toward the world and the face of God." *Of Grammatology*, trans. Gayatri Charravorty Spivak (Baltimore: Johns Hopkins University Press, 1976), p. 13. Also: "The age of the sign is essentially theological." *Grammatology*, p. 14.

7. *Grammatology*, p. 49.

8. *Grammatology*, p. 50.

9. *Grammatology*, p. 315.

10. *Grammatology*, p. 24.

11. Jacques Derrida, *Positions*, trans. Alan Bass (Chicago: University of Chicago Press, 1981), p. 93.

12. *Positions*, p. 94.

13. *Positions*, p. 81.

14. *Grammatology*, p. 314.

15. Jacques Derrida, "The Supplement of the Copula," in Josué Harari, ed., *Textual Strategies, in Post-Structuralist Criticism* (Ithaca: Cornell University Press, 1979), p. 109.

16. Michel Foucault, "What is an Author?" in Harari, p. 159.

17. Michel Foucault, *The Order of Things* (New York, Random House, 1970), p. 34.

18. *Order of Things*, p. 35.

19. Michel Foucault, *Madness and Civilization*, trans. Richard Howard (New York: Random House, 1965), pp. 115–16.

20. *Madness and Civilization*, p. 108.

21. Michel Foucault, *Power/Knowledge*, trans. Colin Gordon et. al. (New York: Pantheon Books, 1980), p. 119.

22. *Power/Knowledge,* p. 59.

23. Michel Foucault, *The History of Sexuality,* vol. 1, trans. Robert Hurley (New York: Random House, 1980), p. 101.

24. *Order of Things,* p. 341.

25. *Order of Things,* p. 375.

26. James Hillman, *The Dream and the Underworld* (New York: Harper & Row, 1979), p. 45.

27. Jacques Derrida, "The Question of Style," in David Allison, ed., *The New Nietzsche* (New York: Delta Books, 1977), p. 179.

28. Jacques Derrida, *Spurs,* trans. Barbara Harlow (Chicago: University of Chicago Press, 1979), p. 39.

29. See the essay "The Novel as Polylogue" in Julia Kristeva, *Desire in Language* (New York: Columbia University Press, 1980).

2

CHARLES E. WINQUIST

Body, Text, and Imagination

God is a questioning of God?
REB ARWAS

(EDMOND JABÉS, *The Book of Questions*)

I

In 1896 Freud published a paper examining the etiology of the neuroses in which he first used the word *psycho-analysis* to describe a method of investigation that inaugurated discursive patterns marking the beginning of a trail into an imaginal reality and imaginal body. "Travelling backwards into the patient's past, step by step, and always guided by the organic train of symptoms and of memories and thoughts aroused, I finally reached the starting-point of the pathological process; and I was obliged to see that at bottom the same thing was present in all the cases submitted to analysis—the action of an agent which must be accepted as the specific cause of hysteria. . . . The event of which the subject has retained an unconscious memory is a *precocious experience of sexual relations with actual excitement of the genitals, resulting from sexual abuse committed by another person.*"[1]

In 1897 Freud wrote a letter to Wilhelm Fliess in which he confessed, "I no longer believe in my *neurotica*."[2] It was the necessary action of the agent, the event with *actual* excitement of the genitals, that he no longer believed in. "It is curious that I feel not in the least disgraced, though the occasion might seem to require it. Certainly I shall not tell it in Gath, or publish it in the streets of Askalon, in the land of the Philistines—but between ourselves I have a feeling more of triumph than of defeat (which cannot be right)."[3] That curious sense of triumph accompanied a further step toward the recognition of the text of the imaginal body.

In 1918 Freud published the case history of the "Wolf Man." Through a dazzling display of analytical virtuosity he uncovers a primal scene at the heart of this obsessional neurosis. He then says: "I should myself be glad to know whether the primal scene in my present patient's case was a phantasy or a real experience; but, taking other similar cases into account, I must admit that the answer to this question is not in fact a matter of very great importance."[4]

A very important development occurred in psychoanalytic discourse between the paper of 1896 and the publication of the case history of the "Wolf Man." Freud deepened his grasp of the textuality of psychological experience and expanded the boundaries of what was psychoanalytically possible to say. The body expressed itself in the text of memory and the text became its own body. It mattered less and less whether the experience of the body of the text was historically congruent with the experience of the physical body. It was the image of the body, the imaginal body, the body of the text, that was the prime material constructed and transformed by healing psychoanalytical narrative. Freud experientially deconstructed the epistemological frame holding the metaphor of language as the mirror of nature. It is probably his self-analysis that cleared the space for an interpretation of dreams as a paradigm for cultural representation that is always subject to disguise, distortion, displacement, and stereotyped symbolization. The base material, the text of the phenomenal world, is given as an impure text representing the body.

Psychoanalysis began as a "talking cure." It began with a text and not with a *tabula rasa*. The markings on the given tablet are always of an uncertain origin because they do not materially correspond with what they represent. The markings are present and that presence announces an absence of what is represented that is also a difference from what is represented. What Freud discovered in his fantasies and in the fantasies of his patients was a crisis in our relationship to language. Language was not a mirror of nature that established an identity. It was a reduplication of nature that established a difference. Words can be objects but they are not the objects they represent. It is in the gap defined by this difference that Freud delivered a wound to the light metaphors of consciousness and the mirror metaphors of language.

Freud is not the only philosopher of suspicion who has delivered a wound to the root metaphors of Western epistemology. Marx and Nietzsche are often cited for their contribution to this philosophical upheaval. Recently, Richard Rorty has elegantly argued that the epistemic privilege of mirror images has been laid to waste in the Anglo-American tradition and that it is time for a philosophy without mirrors, a move from epistemology to hermeneutics.[5] Although the wound inflicted on consciousness and language is not a singular achievement of Freud, it is especially interesting in Freud because he senses a triumph in inflicting the wound to his own theory. More importantly he stays with the body and the sexual etiology of the neuroses. What is changed is the body. It is the reduplicated body of the text that is important and subject to psychoanalytic augmentation and intervention. The body of the text is a subtle body, metaphorical and polymorphic. It is possible that it is this new body that Freud was sensing in his affirmation to Fliess. The metaphorical construction of the body in a semantics of meaning is not limited to physiological possibilities or historical probabilities. Its importance and sexuality can be disseminated throughout the whole semantic realm by wordplay in a system of intertextual references. The signifier was freed from its biological limitations. What was sexual could become psychosexual and what became psychosexual could become all of culture through a linguistic imperialism mobilized by concepts of defense and sublimation. These concepts, as was pointed out by Harold Bloom, correspond to rhetorical tropes.[6] Freud cleared semantic space by his map of misreading for the dissemination of the body throughout the whole of culture.

II

The shattering of the mirror of language denies a privileged representation of the body in a semantic field, but it does not deny the representation of the body that is a reduplication. This body, however, is not limited and is not always recognizable as body. It is this body that Freud extended into all cultural achievements and that I am identifying as the body of the text. It is not just the text but the sensuality of the text that is its subtle body. Since the body that is represented falls outside of its representation, the subtle body of the text is a presence of what is absent. Its sensuality depends upon that presence and its subtlety upon the absence. We are talking about two bodies and one body. Their relationship is part of the enigma of our beginning.

The two bodies are not identical but there is a play between them, and because of that playful dialectic we sense a unity that is always appearing and disappearing. Our beginning is an act and not a text but it is an act that appears only in the text. We are restricted to the text because it is what appears in the assignment of meaning to the play. The play of meaning in a language-game is a familiar metaphor since Wittgenstein introduced this concept in his *Philosophical Investigations.* "Here the term 'language-*game*' is meant to bring into prominence the fact that the *speaking* of language is part of an activity, or a form of life."[7] He later says that "the meaning of a word is its use in language."[8] The activity, the form of life, the use in language all seem closer to our experience of textuality than the mirror image of the world or ourselves. The mirror has no support or meaning outside of the language-game.

The semantic achievement is not perceptual. Only if we

stood in close proximity to objects as we were naming them and accompanied the naming with a pointing gesture might we sustain the metaphor of the mirror image. As soon as we distance ourselves and defer the meaning, we immediately note a difference. The deferring is a differing. We are playing a game that is not governed by the primacy of perception. The rules that govern the game are the rules of discourse. Perception notes a discontinuity through the deferral. The word *dog* does not look like a dog, sound like a dog, or feel like a dog. This semantic *dog* is accessible to a whole world of meanings; it is pliable; it can be transformed. This accession into language can be a multiplication of meaning but it is also a loss of the presence of the dog in the economy of its world of natural forces. All of our talk about the dog has been a transformation of force into meaning. We mark a difference not at the beginning but in the deferral.

We should not, however, think that we can recover an identity with experience that is not already different from itself because every return is but another deferral. We can only throw a fleeting glance at a beginning through the theater of memory already burdened with the multiplication of meanings. We find meaning when we search for force, but this repetition of meaning within the game may be a clue to the beginning that eludes our grasp. That is, the search for a beginning is the repetition of the beginning. We constantly try to repeat life in a more accessible form.[9] We cannot grasp the beginning so we *begin* the search for the beginning. When we are awash with meanings, we experience the absence of our achievement. Our achievement is the repression of force. The language-game is the substitution of a cultural world of meanings, controlled and accessible, for the lost, seething, tumbling disorder of forces that molest our memories. Language can only tell the tale of the origination of its speech in the space of its achievement; and, there, it simply marks an absence. That is, its mark is an absence of the force it represents.

We see this activity written small in a story that Freud

relates about a young boy of one and one-half years of age.[10] The boy could say only a few comprehensible words and make a few sounds that were intelligible to those around him. He was a good little boy except for a habit of throwing his toys away. He made a sound as he threw his toys that both Freud and the boy's mother thought represented the German word *fort* (gone). Freud said that he later noticed that the boy played a game with a wooden reel and a string. He would throw the reel and make a sound that approximated *fort*. After the reel disappeared he would pull the string until it returned and say *da* (there). The child found great satisfaction in this game of *fort-da*. It was a game that reduplicated and repeated the theme of disappearance and return. "The interpretation of the game then became obvious. It was related to the child's great cultural achievement—the instinctual renunciation (that is, the renunciation of instinctual satisfaction) he had made in allowing his mother to go away without protesting. He compensated himself for this, as it were, by himself staging the disappearance and return of the objects within his reach."[11] The little boy gained mastery over the turbulent forces that accompanied the temporary loss of his mother by reduplicating the loss in a game that had rules that guaranteed the return of the lost object.

Freud used this illustration to talk about the motives that lead children to play. He thought that most theories up to this time failed to bring the *economic* motive to the foreground. There is a yield of pleasure that accompanies the play.[12] The aesthetics of play is complemented by this economic consideration. *Fort-da* reduplicates rather than mirrors the disappearance-appearance of the mother so that the child has control over his created world and receives pleasure from it. The game is overdetermined in the realm of force but not in the realm of forces that determine the mother's behavior. There is a sensuality in the text of the child's game, but because of the real absence of the mother it should be clear that "the pleasure of the text is irreducible to physiological need."[13] Physiological needs are woven through the spaces of the text in the satisfaction of mixed discourse so that this satisfaction is not simply semantic or economic. The satisfaction is a dialectical achievement that is approximated in the appearance of the text before it disappears behind the materiality of the text.

The dialectic is a double loss and a double gain, and the sensuality of the text that is its satisfaction lies in the breaches constituted by the complexity of these multiple actions. The first loss corresponds with the first gain. A signifier in the semantic realm is substituted for a force in our physiological or physical economy. The loss or repression of force in this substitution is at the same time a gain in meaning—a semantic connectedness. The reel and string are substituted for the mother. The word is substituted for the body. The reel and string are subject to the laws of *fort-da*. There is mastery and meaning in the game but the game itself corresponds with the loss or disappearance of the mother. Freud does not say, but it can be easily imagined from our own experiences that the satisfaction in the production of meaning in the game could be great enough that even when the mother reappears the game could go on, and her reappearance could now be an intrusion. Many of us have held onto the seduction of the subtle body of the text to the exclusion of the physiological body. In fact, even my talk of the physiological body is already a representation and a repression.

This enigma is an aspect of the second loss and gain which together are a coincidental antinomy with the first loss and gain. The appearance of the text is the display or the gain of a new materiality. That is, the text has an ontic status. It stands materially in the realm of force and this materiality is not contained in the meaning that is the first gain in the transformation of force into meaning. The presence of meaning requiring the materiality of the text, sound or inscription, has, in its representation of what is now absent, established a new presence in the economy of forces that is itself not represented in the semantics of meaning. The text can never exhaust its potential for meaning through multiplication or repetition because it always establishes a material presence that eludes the range of what is immediately reduplicated, since this immediate presence is in the realm of an economics of force. The materiality or fabric of the text is a sensuous weave precisely because it is never what it appears to be. It never contains itself.

There is something uncanny about the text because of the coincidental antinomy. We are used to the first experience of gain and loss. Through it we create a world that is intelligible. It is a world that can be mastered, repeated, and expanded. But, as we travel through this created world, sometimes we miss a connection, and much like a traveler sitting in a train station after missing a connection, we note the detailed materiality of what is around us. If it is a long wait, everything—the walls, the chairs, the doors, the scattered newspapers—becomes oppressive in its presence. It doesn't fit into a narrative. We missed a connection and suddenly have to account for what appears and not what it means. This material reflexivity presses on us whenever we miss a connection. The waiting is a beginning. We feel that we have to make sense out of the materiality of what appears. We have to make sense out of the materiality of the text.

Artists, poets, and novelists disturb the popular imagination when their work becomes materially reflexive. When the text becomes a reflection on textuality, when painting or sculpture presents its medium as its subject rather than using the medium to represent what it is not, there is a representation of secondary gain and loss. The paradox is that the missed connection becomes the first connection to inaugurate a repression of force and proliferation of meaning. What defies our expectation is that we cannot go back to the first text after we have missed a connection. The supplement that comes out of this breach has altered the economy of forces that was represented in the first text. The supplement transgresses the first text and is irreducible to the first text since the supplement has its own originality. We know of no absolute text that lies behind present texts. All we know are present texts and all that we can say that lies behind a text is the scene of its origination. That scene can be represented only in a new text. Even if we think we are getting behind a text we are not at the same time getting behind textuality.

Secondary loss and gain can be simply illustrated in Freud's example of the *fort-da* game. The gain in control and meaning in the substitution of the reel and string for the loss of the mother is supplemented by the material instrumentality of the reel and string. The reel and string are the material possibility for the representational substitution and mastery of *fort-da* in controlling the meaning of the disappearance-appearance of the mother. There is a gain in meaning and control but also a gain in materiality that is a loss of meaning and control. The game works as long as the string does not break, the reel remains tied to the string, or there are no obstacles to the retrieval of the reel. The materiality of the text of this game introduces a different set of forces from those mastered in compensation for the disappearance of the mother.

The game repeated life in a more accessible form for the child and all works well until the string breaks. The broken string would be a missed connection that halts the flow of meaning. The first experience of the child would not be fresh display of new meanings but a grief over the loss of meaning. The forces that control the action of the reel and string are not meaningful in the text of *fort-da*. The break of the string and the breach of the text would be an intrusion of what are again untamed forces. The text would remain overdetermined in an economics of force, but pleasure would give way to anger and anxiety. The attention of the child would be focused on the materiality of the reel and string and not on the meaning generated in the game. Probably anger would be directed toward the broken object and then anxiety would surround the broken text.

The double determination, the double gain, and the double loss are the risks that accompany every game and every text. No text can be complete and authorized because it is always more than it appears to be. No text can be exhaustively true and every text is sensual. Texts cannot escape their materiality. This is a part of the text that is opaque. The double determination also means that there are at least two edges to the text. That is, the text is duplex. It speaks a duplicity. When connections are missed the seams in the fabric of the text show. Sometimes the surface garment gapes and we witness the sensuous surface of the text. These moments are not themselves filled with meaning but are the loss of meaning and the space for meaning. The commitment to understanding the givenness of experience places us before these appearances. We do not here have a foundation but we do have a beginning. The saving of the appearances is a saving of the text/image or, we might even say, a saving of the imagination. We must talk about the imagination because the text is never only literal. It is event as well as content. There is a scene of origination. As much as we might want to get behind that scene to a foundation, we have to take account of the scene if we are honest to experience.

III

What appears in language is not nature but the text. The text is not a mirror but a supplement. It has its own presence that breaks with nature, draws away from nature, and establishes its own meaning. Derrida refers to the description of the moving away from nature as having a scene.[14] The very existence of words indicates "a breach with the phenomenality of things."[15] We cannot turn to nature to give an account of the scene of textual origination because the presence of the text is a break or breach that moves away from nature. We also cannot turn to semantics to tell us about the scene of textual origination because the functional relations internal to the text refer only to themselves. The scene is event-ful. The scene is part of a

theater. Telling must be also a showing because it is not just
the appearance of the text but the appearing of the text that
constitutes the scene.

In Freud, the scene of origination, the primal scene, is a
repression that creates and compromises culture at the
same time. The diachronic fantasy of societal origins is
reduplicated in particularized histories of individuals as an
axial reference in the further dissemination of their textual
identity. For Derrida, Freud's primal scene, the breach with
nature, is a scene of writing. "In that moment of world
history 'subsumed' by the name of Freud, by means of an
unbelievable mythology . . . a relationship to itself of the
historico-transcendental stage of writing was spoken
without being said, thought without being thought: was
written and simultaneously erased, metaphorized; designating itself while indicating intraworldly relations, it
was represented."[16] Bloom gives priority to the trespass of
teaching, a scheme of transumption or metaleptic reversal,
that he calls the primal scene of instruction.[17] The great
precursors, absorbed into the cauldron of id forces,
complexify the meaning of Freud's metaphorical beginnings
by incorporating secondary textual gain into the nature that
is breached.

The primal scene is itself the trope of a trope. It is the representation of representation. It doubles the imagination
by imagining imagination. Figures for the transgression of
language are substituted for the transgression of nature.
The assault on language is a reduplication of the assault on
nature. The original act of transforming force into meaning
is metaleptically reversed by turning meaning, convoluting
its achievement, toward the gaps in the textual fabric. The
substitution of the reel and string for the disappearing
mother is brought to immediate awareness by choosing to
break the string. The break with nature was the substitution
of the reel and string for the mother. The way back to the
substitution is by the transgression of the game, breaking
the string. The broken figure sacrifices meaning in an attempt to represent the origination of meaning. Meaning is

brought to force, gives recognition to force but does not itself become force.

The entertainment of troped language approximates a mixed discourse in a semantic display. It references the transformation of experience through the dialectic of presence and absence that makes it no longer identical with itself. The primal scene is always a metaphor. What is unique is that it is a metaphor of metaphoricity. A scene is substituted for an act of disjunction between force and meaning, just as within that act meaning is substituted for force. A scene of substitution is substituted for an act of substitution. There is both a reenactment and a reduplication. There is here a dialectic that is the foundation of mixed discourse. This dialectic is neither language nor force, but it is rooted in force and spread throughout language. The dialectic does not take us behind or below metaphor. It is a delineation of what we mean by metaphor.

This is an expanded view of metaphor, a metaphorical reading of metaphor that turns to discourse instead of to the word or sentence for the unit of determination. The use of metaphor can be a rhetorical strategy within discourse, but more importantly it is the possibility for discourse. Discourse is mimetic of its foundation when it creates meaning through internal substitutions of dissimilar units of nomination. Discourse is itself the substitution of words for forces. This is why discourse is always mixed and indeterminate. A necessary ambiguity lies in the wake of discursive achievements because of their metaphorical structure. Literalism is an illusion. What we mean by meaning requires both substitution and difference. To give meaning to an experience is to alter the experience through primary and secondary loss and gain. For example, *putting* something into words and *putting* something into type are progressive substitutions that are determinate only by their own presence. Only if language were a mirror and discourse a mirroring could we posit a literalism. Discourse is a dialectical work or metaphorical movement. It makes a difference. We are makers of meaning.

There is a tension in this insight. The making of meaning is at the same time a loss. Force is repressed as force in order to be accessible as meaning. Meaning is both an achievement and an alienation. We have recognized here that the world of meaning is a mediated achievement amidst immediate forces. Life hangs over the gap between meaning and force. It is in the space of this gap that we sense a surplus of meaning or metaphorical potential for the further determination of meaning. It is also in the space of this gap that there is room for the return of the repressed. Discourse continually passes through this space but the direction of its movement is variable. The metaphorical potential of discourse allows it to move from force to meaning or to bring meaning to force. These are different movements and not simply a change in direction. The creation of meaning is a repression through active substitution. The movement of meaning to force is not a substitution but a subversion of language achievements that is possible because of secondary gains in the creation of meaning. The subversion is a deconstruction of the material instrumentality needed for the substitution for the making of meaning. We can subvert the game of *fort-da* by breaking the string that connects to the reel. We can subvert a language-game by troping the conventional patterns that hold together its disparate parts. There is no single or ideal task for discourse. Each discipline of the imagination will have to create a genre of mixed discourse to fulfil its metaphorical potential and to determine the direction of its movement.

The history of every imaginal discipline will be a history of movements: starts, false starts, grand journeys, and reversals. It is usually only at times of crisis that there is an awareness that the metaphorical potential of discourse is indeterminate. When movement slows or is paralyzed a reversal of former movements is possible. The discipline hesitates in the recognition of the ambiguity of its own possibilities. The crisis that ensues is usually thought to be a crisis of meaning or values that reside in particular patterns of meaning when, in fact, what we are experiencing is a larger crisis in our relationship with language. Discourse is mixed and has only one of its feet planted in the realm of semantic achievement. When the semantic achievement falters the crisis has begun, but we have not plumbed its depths if we restrict our thinking to the problem of meaning. Deconstruction is as important a movement as reconstruction. The crisis of our relationship to language is, at the same time, the crisis of our relationship to the economic display of force. The problem in assessing the range of possible movements, of course, is that discourse cannot simply reverse itself and talk the economics of force. It speaks and writes in the semantic realm of meanings. It faces the semantic realm.

Deconstruction is dizzying. It is a walking backwards. It is a subversion that is hard to sustain because, at the same time, it is disseminating a new speech that can be multiplied and repeated in the construction of meaning. Of course a contrasting, predominately constructive orientation also evidences the deconstruction of precursor figures and figurations. In deconstructionist thought it is the dominance of a negative capability that distinguishes it from self-consciously constructive thinking. Deconstructive discourse is depressive. It pulls the semantic achievement down toward what was repressed by the very fact of representational origination. The new speech that it disseminates is usually a metalanguage that firms its footing in the semantic realm because the foot placed in the semantically indeterminate realm of force can never be sure of itself.

IV

Deconstructionist thought has deep roots in philosophical structuralist and psychoanalytic sensitivities, but in America it is best known and practiced in circles of literary criticism. There was already a tradition of structuralist criticism and, since "the saving of the text" is a fundamental theme of deconstruction, the immediate application to literary

criticism is obvious. However, the work of deconstructionist literary critics has become very important for understanding the work of all disciplines that work with texts.
The shattering of language as the mirror of nature, insight
into the metaphoricity of all discourse, and other legacies of
deconstructionism alter what most imaginative disciplines
understand as their foundation. Their work cannot proceed
as if untouched on a deep level when the materiality of texts
becomes an impassable passage and the text is at the heart
of the discipline. The aporetic opacity of texts clearly affects
the work of theologians, philosophers, and social scientists.
It is not a problem that can be put aside as somebody else's
problem. The intertwining of body, text, and imagination in
the mask of culture is a problem for thinking that is as
universal as the cultural disguise that covers over our world.
We need to think this problem through in many disciplines
to experience its importance.

The deconstructionist problematic is not the creation of
one group of thinkers. It is the problematic of the text: its
origin in discourse and writing, the materiality of its
presence, and its relationship to the realities it represents.
These are persistent problems that have been well
documented in the histories of philosophy and theology.
They emerge whenever thinking turns on itself and
experiences its textual supplement. Deconstructionism did
not create the problem but it displays a negative capability
in its retrograde reflections, or pertinences for a new
discursivity that can generate a literature that is yet untried
in much philosophical and theological thinking or in the
social sciences.

Theology is a particularly interesting discipline to look at
in relationship to deconstructionist themes because it has
clearly witnessed a crisis in its relationship with language.
The ferment in theology from the early sixties has been a
persistent discussion of the possibility for theological
language. The question that occupied the center of
theological reflection over the past two decades was not
about the validity of theological language but it was about

the meaning or meaninglessness of theological language. Theology questioned its own possibility.

The eclipse of God, the disappearance of God, and the death of God became serious discussions when the material instrumentality of theological discourse was experienced as disconnected from any reference in the real world. In 1969, Langdon Gilkey retrospectively asserted that the fundamental question asked by the new theologians was a very different question from the questions asked by their liberal and neoorthodox teachers. "Is there in experience any transcendent dimension for which religious or theological language is necessary and in relation to which it makes sense?"[18] That question in its various forms of expression had the power to break the literal connectedness of theology with the world it had claimed to represent. The missed connection, the broken string, and the death of God coalesce in this image and bring to our minds the deconstructionist reminder of the materiality of the text. The child's game of *fort-da* mastering the disappearance of the mother uncomfortably parallels the theological language-game mastering the disappearance of God. What is important is that both games take on a new significance when the string is broken or a connection is missed.

Theology must stop and look around at its own semantic achievement when experience can no longer sustain the literal connection between theology's words and the world it represents. Theology is not a mirror. It is writing and writing is a substitution and a repression. Theology represents a world but the connection is not literal. Like all other disciplines of the imagination its scene of origination is metaphorical. Perhaps theology always knew that it was metaphorical as it led readers through the labyrinth of a dark night of the soul, or up the sides of magical mountains or into the complexities of an inner *verbum*. Maybe it always disguised its second order of reflection in the first-order display of the world it claimed to represent or even present. Now, after self-inflicted wounds it must take account of the semantic achievement that is its construction.

The emphasis on construction in theology immediately comes up against the metaphor of deconstruction. Its texts are rich and varied. Theology has not restricted its questions or limited the domain of its inquiry. Even after its confrontation with meaninglessness, it continues to talk of transcendence, ultimate horizons, and eschatological disclosures. It continues to construct worlds under horizons of hope, freedom, and love. Sometimes it rewrites history as a prolepsis of apocalyptic happenings. It talks not only of presence but of total presence. In general, it now self-consciously constructs a world using a limit-language.

Gordon Kaufman in *An Essay on Theological Method* writes that "Theology . . . is fundamentally an activity of *construction* (and reconstruction) not of description or exposition, as it has ordinarily understood in the past; and the failure to grasp this fact has led to mistaken expectations for theology and to the use of misleading criteria both in doing theology and in assessing its conclusions."[19] He says that when we recognize that theology is a constructive activity, "it becomes clear that the central problem of theological method is to discern and formulate explicit criteria and procedures for theological construction."[20] How does this assertion of the central methodological problem of theology relate to deconstructionism? This is not an isolated question to be directed to Kaufman's work alone. Serious postcritical theologies have generally acknowledged the overdetermination of meaning and the function of the imagination in theological construction. They have accepted responsibility for the making of meaning in theological thinking. Philosophical hermeneutics has helped shape a theopoetic sensibility that has revitalized traditional theological work. Theology rescued itself from the museum through a metaanalysis of the second order that saved the text from an incredulous literalism and saved the text for imaginative construction. Second-order theology is a multiplication of meaning that returns the text to the work of theology.

The work is still to be done. Kaufman is again very

helpful in locating the problem by calling for us to "recognize both the possibility and appropriateness of a third-order theology."[21] "That is, acknowledging that all theological positions are rooted fundamentally in imaginative construction (second-order theology), we must now take control (so far as possible) of our theological activity and attempt deliberately to construct our concepts and images of God and the world; and then we must seek to see human existence in terms of these symbolical constructions."[22] If deconstructionism is to have a place in theology it will be in this third order that is yet to be determined. What is placed before us is the decision of how to take control of the theological task. At first glance, deconstructionist thinking would reverse the direction suggested by Kaufman; but, we must remind ourselves of the complex dialectic of metaphorical loss and gain before we harden this assessment. Deconstructionist thinking should be examined as an available option for third-order theology even when the task is first envisioned as a constructive task.

V

Third-order theology begins with the textual legacy of first- and second-order theologies. How do we *take control* of our activity in the midst of the texts that constitute this legacy? How do we choose to stand in relationship to these texts? How do we do theology in this crowded marketplace of established meanings?

Whatever else may characterize third-order theology, we know that it will be a hermeneutic of texts. Otherwise it would be of the first or second orders. The problem of starting is deciding what we do following the postcritical relinquishment of descriptive literalism. The experience of the text and textuality block even sophisticated appeals to romantic primitivisms with attendant literalisms that call us back to the Bible, back to nature, or back to origins. These are all too easily seen as diachronic fantasies elaborated from textual achievements to be taken seriously as an escape from the responsibility of third-order theology. What we see is that instead of being taken behind the text, the text expands. A new text confronts us that supplements our beginning reflection, and we are again faced with the question of how to do theology.

The problem of how to begin a third-order theology is clearer when we acknowledge that second-order theology is a permanent dislocation of the dreams of Enlightenment rationalism for a replication of nature in the mirror of language and that it is not a wound that can be healed. The dream has been dislocated from the center of thinking. It is one dream beside others. We begin with metaphor, talk about metaphor metaphorically, and recognize every closure as a metaphorical achievement. Third-order theology must be self-consciously a mixed discourse. The beginning is fluid. The texts cannot dictate our response. That is, the work is between the spaces of past achievements, and how we move is not yet determined. This is why we can talk about taking control of theological activity. There is a tension in every metaphor, a conflict in every interpretation and a conflict between interpretations.

We are in a privileged space of overdetermination touching both force and meaning. It is a hermeneutical field. The achievements are duplex and show themselves in their duplicity. As Paul Ricoeur has shown, we can work expansively toward the recollection and restoration of meaning[23] or we can shape interpretation as an exercise of suspicion.[24] Both moves can work within the metaphoricity of language and both moves recognize the mythopoetic core of the imagination.

The hermeneutics of expansion is an exegetical work. It repeats the text and multiplies its meaning in a supplementary expansion throughout the semantic realm. This is the option that Kaufman describes when he suggests that we construct concepts and images of God and the world and then disseminate them broadly so that we see human existence in relationship to these constructions. In contrast, the hermeneutics of suspicion is transgressive. It violates the text by forcing it back on its materiality, by perforating its surface achievement with questions that direct us to what the text is not, by troping patterns of internal coherence, and by stretching connections to the breaking point.

The hermeneutics of expansion recognizes in the metaphoricity of discourse the opportunity for unrestricted elaboration in the semantic realm. Every text can be lifted up into a more complex pattern of meaning or recollected under a larger horizon. Theology can become a phenomenology of the spirit "in which each figure finds its meaning, not in what precedes but in what follows."[25] Theology can elaborate the subtle body of the text so that it envelopes the semantic world. Once language is no longer viewed as a mirror of nature, there are only internal controls on definitional complexity. A lexical hierarchy can be generated by progressive substitution and repression until an all-encompassing concept by "that than which nothing greater can be conceived" stands abstractly in relationship to all other concepts and images. God can be created semantically through metaphorical gain. We might even say that the concept of God is the teleological fulfillment of the metaphorical potential in discourse. "God is a questioning of God."

The deconstruction within a hermeneutics of suspicion is also a discursive achievement. It creates a supplementary text, but this text transgresses rather than augments the meaning of received texts. Patterns of interference create spaces in and between the texts, and the spaces are more highly valued than the text. Spaces isolate texts and cast them adrift on the seam of forces. Language is sometimes contracted or condensed so that the supplementary text intends silence. Rhetorical tropes are combined to hide connections and force the textual images to stand in front of us by themselves in a space cleared by disguise. The missed connections delay representation and the material presence of the image is mute.

The semantic activity in deconstructionist discourse is variable and always particular. Language can be pushed so far that it transgresses the limits of intelligibility; meaning disappears, and we are left with the materiality of speech or writing. The elision of principal parts of ordinary discourse hints at the achievement of meaning but again only displays the materiality of discourse. The introduction of dissimilar constructions into narrative progressions stops the expected flow, turns discourse, and clears the space where we had anticipated the establishment of meaning. The collision or overlay of dissimilar texts will often cancel out parts and isolate images that claim our attention and draw us into their extralinguistic isolation. Graphological displacements can also subvert the flow of meaning and leave us with a naked text.

Deconstructionist thought explicitly or implicitly interrogates the text. The different styles of inquiry all establish a practical method to attend to the importance of questions that violate the semantic framework in which they are enclosed. This violation is at the same time a recognition of language as naturally symbolic and discourse as the path between meaning and force. We can cross the path in either direction.

Deconstructionist theological discourse tries to pull the text back toward the economics of force. It is a depressive movement that subverts the horizontal semantic display. It is a constant reminder of the metaphor that gives textual body to physical body. We step back into the forces of the imagination as we prescind from its achievement.

For deconstructionist theology, third-order theological construction can be incorporated into its agenda along with first- and second-order semantic achievements. Even its own textual achievement is subject to further work. It continually reverses the semantic flow and folds language back upon itself. The text is a momentary closure and the text can always be deconstructed. The project has no closure. Representation always announces an absence. The most elaborate theological constructions are empty of everything but their own material presence. Theological constructions need the deconstruction that pulls them back toward the economics of force. They must be constantly plumbed for their metaphorical roots if they are to remain fecund. "God is a questioning of God" is interesting because it represents an absence, has a mute sensuality, and is the transcendence of a body of experience. Deconstruction gives significance to meaning.

VI

Construction and deconstruction are complementary but not coincidental strategies of third-order theology. They work with texts and disseminate texts that constitute the subtle body of subjective experience. Together they intertwine force and meaning so that experiencing their complementarity is not a task to be carried to resolution. There is no resolution. There is instead a tension and complex dialectic that, when it is represented, is a reduplication of the metaphoricity of language. A unified search for the meaning of third-order theology would require a reductionist interpretation that is forgetful of its metaphorical beginnings and is repressive of the economics of force. The simple proliferation of texts will establish meanings, but these meanings will have to be allowed to interfere with one another as part of a dialectical interchange between force and meaning that works because of textual and intertextual absences in the semantic realm. Every text can be elaborated and transgressed. Every text is a pre-text in relationship to future texts and, at the same time, the residue of the scene of its origination. However the text is taken up in future discourse, it brings with it a meaning that is the work of repression and substitution.

As we deepen our grasp on the textuality of theological experience and expand the boundaries of what is theologically possible to say, we, as Freud, will work with the subtle body of the text as a substitute for the text of the body. We cannot escape the deferral of desire in the scene of origination. The theology of the future, theology of the third order, is a theology of desire.

NOTES

1. Sigmund Freud, *The Standard Edition of the Complete Psychological Works of Sigmund Freud*, 24 vols. (London: Hogarth Press and the Institute of Psychoanalysis, 1953–1974). Vol. 3, pp. 151–52 (hereafter referred to as SE).

2. Sigmund Freud, *The Origins of Psychoanalysis: Letters to Wilhelm Fliess* (New York: Basic Books, 1954), p. 215.

3. *Origins,* p. 217.

4. SE 17, p. 97.

5. Cf. Richard Rorty, *Philosophy and the Mirror of Nature* (Princeton: Princeton University Press, 1979).

6. Harold Bloom, *A Map of Misreading* (New York: Oxford University Press, 1975), p. 84.

7. Ludwig Wittgenstein, *Philosophical Investigations* (Oxford: Basil Blackwell, 1967), p. 11.

8. Wittgenstein, p. 20.

9. Cf. Edward Said, *Beginnings: Intention and Method* (Baltimore: Johns Hopkins University Press, 1975), p. 89.

10. SE 18, pp. 14–17.

11. SE 18, p. 14.

12. SE 18, p. 14.

13. Roland Barthes, *The Pleasure of the Text* (New York: Hill and Wang, 1975), p. 17.

14. Jacques Derrida, *Of Grammatology,* trans. Gayatri Chakravorty Spivak (Baltimore: Johns Hopkins University Press, 1974), p. 151.

15. Geoffrey H. Hartman, *Saving the Text* (Baltimore: Johns Hopkins University Press, 1981), p. xvi.

16. Jacques Derrida, *Writing and Differences,* trans. Alan Bass (Chicago: University of Chicago Press, 1978), pp. 228–29.

17. Bloom, pp. 32, 49.

18. Langdon Gilkey, *Naming the Whirlwind: The Renewal of God-Language* (Indianapolis: Bobbs-Merrill, 1969), p. 13.

19. Gordon D. Kaufman, *An Essay on Theological Method* (Missoula, Mont.: Scholars Press, 1979), p. x.

20. Kaufman, p. 36.

21. Kaufman, p. 38.

22. Kaufman, p. 38.

23. Paul Ricoeur, *Freud and Philosophy: An Essay on Interpretation,* trans. Denis Savage (New Haven: Yale University Press, 1970), pp. 28–32.

24. Ricoeur, pp. 32–36.

25. Paul Ricoeur, *The Conflict of Interpretations* (Evanston: Northwestern University Press, 1974), p. 21.

3

MARK C. TAYLOR

Text as Victim

The poem of the mind in the act of finding
What will suffice. It has not always had
To find: the scene was set; it repeated what
Was in the script.
                  Then the theatre was changed
To something else. Its past was a souvenir.
It had to be living, to learn the speech of the place.
WALLACE STEVENS

The stage is theological for as long as it is dominated by
speech, by a will to speech, by the layout of a primary logos
which does not belong to the theatrical site and governs it
from a distance. The stage is theological for as long as its
structure, following the entirety of tradition, comports the
following elements: an author-creator who, absent and from
afar, is armed with a text and keeps watch over, assembles,
regulates the time or the meaning of the representation,
letting this latter *represent* him as concerns what is called the
content of his thoughts, his intentions, his ideas. He lets
representation represent him through representatives, direc-
tors or actors, enslaved interpreters who represent characters
who, primarily through what they say, more or less directly
represent the thought of the "creator." Interpretive slaves
who faithfully execute the providential designs of the
"master."
JACQUES DERRIDA

LE SOUFFLEUR SOUFFLÉ

On 5 March 1843 an article entitled "Who is the author of
Either-Or?" appeared in the Danish paper *Faedrelandet*. The

58

identity of the author of this essay about authorship was concealed behind the elliptical signature "A. F. . . . ." The distance of nearly a century and a half creates an "acoustic illusion" which appears to enable us to hear Kierkegaard's voice sounding through these tangled lines. But things were not so simple in 1843, and perhaps even today the k-nots in Ariadine's thread cannot be undone so easily.

When *Either-Or* first appeared, few people knew who its author was. The work, which does not bear Kierkegaard's own name, is supposed to have been edited by Victor Eremita. Although apparently intended to clarify the issue of authorship, Victor's editorial preface actually is calculated to complicate the question of the author. In a scathing satire on Hegelian philosophy, Victor explains that one day in a fit of anger he had smashed his treasured desk with a hatchet. The devastating blow uncovered a secret drawer which contained a collection of papers. Victor clearly implies that had it not been for his act of violence, the words we are about to read never would have come to light. Meticulously following the most responsible methods of textual analysis, Victor concludes that the papers he had accidentally discovered were the work of two authors. A collection of "aesthetic essays of varying length," as well as a number of "aphorisms, lyrical effusions, and reflections" all appeared to have been written by an anonymous young man. Two long, carefully argued ethical treatises, presented in the form of epistles addressed to this young man, were signed by a civil magistrate named Judge Wilhelm. Victor explains that "If I were to confine myself strictly to this data, and decide to call him Wilhelm, I should lack a corresponding designation for the first author, and should have to give him an arbitrary name. Hence I have preferred to call the first author A, the second B."[1] Even if *our* questions about authorship have not been fully answered, Victor appears to have settled the issue to his satisfaction.

Just when he seems to have resolved his editorial dilemma, however, Victor stumbles on further puzzles. A does not acknowledge himself as the author, but only as the editor of the longest and most interesting work among "his" papers, *Diary of the Seducer*. In an effort to save his hypothesis about the authorship of the manuscript he is attempting to decipher, Victor suggests that A's disclaimer is nothing more than "an old trick of the novelist." To support his position, Victor points to "evident" continuities between *Diary of the Seducer* and other works by the "same author," most notably *The Immediate Stages of the Erotic* and *Shadowgraphs*. The argument, however, is unconvincing and doubts persist in the mind of the reader. Moreover Victor's answer gives rise to a further chain of questions. If A were the author of the *Diary*, though he insisted otherwise, then could not the papers of A and B have been written by the same person—perhaps by A, perhaps by B, perhaps by neither A nor B? Indeed, Victor is driven to entertain such a disturbing possibility.

> During my constant occupation with the papers, it dawned on me that they might be looked at from a new point of view, by considering all of them as the work of one person. I know very well everything that can be urged against this view, that it is unhistorical, improbable, unreasonable, that one person should be the author of both parts, although the reader might easily be tempted to the wordplay that one who says A must also say B. However, I have not yet been able to give up this idea. Let us imagine a person who had lived through both of these movements, or who had reflected upon both movements. A's papers contain multiple efforts to formulate an aesthetic life-view. A coherent aesthetic view of life can scarcely be rendered. B's papers contain an ethical life-view. As I let this thought sink into my soul, it became clear to me that I might make use of it in choosing a title. The one I have selected expresses precisely this.[2]

This conclusion merely restates the question we have been pursuing from the beginning. If, as the title now seems to suggest, *Either-Or* is the work of a single author, then we want to know the identity of that author. Victor, of course, does not tell us. But he leaves traces for us to follow.

Perhaps it is Victor himself who is employing the "old trick of the novelist" which he accuses A of having used. Perhaps his editorship is the mask behind which he conceals his authorship. Perhaps his apparent search for the author(s) really represents a diversionary tactic. Perhaps. But we cannot be sure.

What does seem certain is that Victor's preface which appears to be an attempt to solve the problem of the authorship of *Either-Or* actually seeks to pose the question of the author. Rather than *an author*, we discover a seemingly endless chain, an infinite proliferation of authors. Authors within authors, or as Victor puts it, "one author seems to be enclosed in another, like the parts in a Chinese puzzle box."[3] And all, perhaps, authored by an author who is, after all, pseudonymous. Victor's preface, it seems, creates "a space into which the writing subject constantly disappears."[4]

With the disappearance of the author, the problem of the text surfaces anew. Not only does *Either-Or* not seem to have *an* author, it is not even *a* text. To the contrary, it is a plurality of texts, texts within texts, texts which overlap, interlace, echo one another. "Every text," in other words, "is the intertext of another text."[5] The plurality of the text "does not mean just that it has several meanings, but rather that it achieves plurality of meaning, an *irreducible* plurality. The Text is not coexistence of meanings but passage, traversal; thus it answers not to an interpretation, liberal though it may be, but to an explosion, a dissemination. The Text's plurality does not depend on the ambuiguity of its contents, but rather on what could be called the *stereographic plurality* of the signifiers that weave it (etymologically the text is a cloth; *textus*, from which text derives, means 'woven')."[6]

Authorial and textual plurality create a labyrinth from which there appears to be no exit, generate works which end, "without result." Author displacing author, text displacing text, and so on, and on, and on. A seemingly endless chain—a chain without clear beginning or definite end. Self-effacing author(s) presenting self-erasing conclusions: Either—Or; either A or B or. . .

And what about Kierkegaard in all of this? He seems to have disappeared behind a series of personae: Victor, A, B, Johannes, and so on. But that is precisely the point (if such a tale can have *a* point). In one of his moments of consistent inconsistency, Kierkegaard deigns to comment on his authorship—a comment which is, significantly, couched in a postscript to his *Postscript* (another chain within a chain?). He explains that his relation to his writings "is even more external than that of a poet, who poetizes characters, and yet in the preface is himself the author. For I am impersonal, or am personal in the second person, a *Souffleur* who has poetically produced the authors, whose preface in turn is their own production, as are even their own names. So in the pseudonymous writings there is not a single word that is mine; I have no opinion about these works except as a reader, not the remotest private relation to them, since such a relation is impossible in the case of a doubly reflected communication."[7] It becomes clear, then, that Kierkegaard understood himself not as an author, but as a *Souffleur*, a prompter whose purpose was to make prompting unnecessary. Like Artaud in our own time, Kierkegaard "wanted the machinery of the prompter [*souffleur*] spirited away [*soufflé*]." The drama created by the play and the interplay of his personae points toward the "conflagration of the stage upon which the prompter was possible and where the body was under the rule of a foreign text."[8]

Le souffleur soufflé—the self-negation of the author which is, paradoxically, the moment of the subject's self-realization. "Writing is now linked to sacrifice and to the sacrifice of life itself; it is a voluntary obliteration of the self that does not require representation in books because it takes place in the everyday existence of the writer. Where a work had the duty of creating immortality, it now attains the right to kill, to become the murderer of its author. Flaubert, Proust, and Kafka [as well as Kierkegaard] are obvious examples of this reversal. In addition, we find the link between writing and death manifested in the total effacement of the individual characteristics of the writer; the quibbling and confrontation that a writer generates between himself and his text cancel out the signs of his particular individuality. If we wish to know the writer in our day, it will be through the singularity of his absence and in his link to death, which has transformed him into a victim of his own writing."[9]

Like Victor Eremita, Kierkegaard leaves us with a(n endless) series of questions: Is there an (A)author? What/Who is an/the (A)author? Is there *a* (T)text? What is a (T)text? Are texts authored or authorless? What/How would authorless texts mean? Who victimizes the (A)author? What is the significance of such sacrifice?

S/TEX(T)UAL TRANSGRESSION

In the course of explaining his relation to his writings, Kierkegaard describes himself as essentially a reader of the works he authored. Here the question of the author turns into the question of the reader. This curious inversion points to a further possibility, a possibility only "indirectly" examined by Kierkegaard. The dialectician must ask: If the author is a reader, then might the reader be an author? Moreover if author is reader and reader author, then is not writing interpretation, or more precisely the interpretation of interpretation? And is not the text the stage or the field upon which the struggle of interpretation is enacted or played? Our problem becomes how to interpret interpretation.

Derrida invites us to "meditate upon all of the following together: writing as the possibility of the road and of difference, the history of writing and the history of the road, of the rupture, of the *via rupta*, of the path that is broken, beaten, *fracta*, of the space of reversibility and of repetition traced by the opening, the divergence from, and the violent spacing of nature, of the natural, savage, salvage, forest. The *silva* is savage, the *via rupta* is written, discerned, and inscribed violently as the difference, as form imposed on the *hyle*, in the forest, in the woods as matter."[10] Writing, roads, inroads, rupture, *via rupta*, broken, beaten, burst, bust, breach, *fracta*, space, spacing, opening, hole, penetrating, *silva*, savage, salvage, strange, uncanny, *umheimlich, hyle,* hymen, matter, *mater*. . . The path Derrida cuts clears a space in which we can explore the question of how to interpret interpretation.

Interpretation is transgression. Transgression is "the action of passing over or beyond." In *The Epistle of St. John,* Maurice explains: "I call it transgression; the passing over of a boundary which was marked out for me." Interpretation takes place on the boundary, at the border, the threshold, the *limen,* betwixt 'n between the settled(ing) and the unsettled(ing), the familiar and the strange, the known and the unknown, the inside and the outside. Interpreters are frontiersmen, limen, pioneers, who "dig trenches, build roads, and perform other labors in clearing and preparing the way for the main body." Voices crying in the wilderness so that some body can come. Pioneers chart "the history of the road, of the rupture, of the *via rupta*, of the path that is broken, beaten, *fracta*. . ."

Ever caught in the "middest," the interpreter never settles, and thus is always unsettling. A wanderer, a sojourner, his "nomad thought"[11] always transgresses, forever passes over, moves beyond in a *ceaseless* struggle to settle the unsettled, familiarize the strange, know the unknown, inwardize the outward. The play of interpretation:

> . . . to eat and to be eaten
> to have the outside inside and to be
> inside the outside.[12]

Inside-out and outside-in—a boundary settlement the interpreter struggles to effect.

For the frontiersman, this settlement is never final. He fails and fails necessarily. In defeat, however, the pioneer touches the nerve of failure and thus no longer must suffer a failure of nerve.[13] The act of interpreting discloses that there is no inside without an outside and no outside without an inside. Foucault correctly maintains that "limit and transgression depend on each other for whatever density of being they possess: a limit could not exist if it were absolutely uncrossable and, reciprocally, transgression would be pointless if it merely crossed a limit composed of illusions and shadows."[14] The oscillating interplay of transgression and limit forms the fabric of the text.

Transgression, of course, is not simply the act of passing over. It is a movement-beyond which violates, penetrates, fractures. To transgress is "to go beyond the bounds or limits prescribed by a law, command, etc.; to break, violate, infringe, contravene, trespass against." Transgression inscribes the *via rupta*. Interpretation is a *hostile* act in which interpreter victimizes text. The followers of Hermes are, after all, thieves (who come in the night?). The effort to settle the unsettled, to familiarize the strange, or to know the unknown is the struggle to possess, to appropriate, to make one's own what had been other. Appropriation culminates in incorporation, the "unity in one body or mass." And as Norman O. Brown points out, "incorporation is eating."[15] The interpreter lives by eating; he sinks his teeth into the text in order to inwardize the outward. Further reflection uncovers a sacrificial dimension of all eating. From this perspective, interpretation appears to be an act of dismemberment in which the text is sacrificed. The *para-doxa* of transgression is that the transgressor *needs* what he sacrifices, is nourished by what he attempts to devour. "Hostilities: our enemy our host, who feeds us; to kill is to eat. Our enemy our host, *hostia*, our Eucharistic meal."[16]

If, however, text is host, then interpretation appears to be parasitical. Transgression, in other words, seems secondary to the primary sacrificial victim. But appearances are deceiving, for in a manner similar to inside and outside, parasite and host are actually symbiotic. Transgression simultaneously reverses and preserves the parasite/host relation by disclosing the *host*-ility of interpretation and the parasitical nature of texts. The *para-doxa* of victimization is that the victim *needs* to be sacrificed, is nourished by being devoured. Host feeds parasite which nourishes host which. . . " 'Para'," J. Hillis Miller explains, "is a double antithetical prefix signifying at once proximity and distance, similarity and difference, interiority and exteriority, something inside a domestic economy and at the same time outside it, something simultaneously this side of a boundary line, threshold, or margin, and also beyond it, equivalent in status and also secondary or subsidiary, submissive, as of guest to host, slave to master. A thing in 'para', moreover, is not only simultaneously on both sides of the boundary line between inside and out. It is also the boundary itself, the screen which is a permeable membrane connecting inside and outside. It confuses them with one another, allowing the outside in, making the inside out, dividing them and joining them. It also forms an ambiguous transition between one and the other."[17]

The recognition of the interplay of host and parasite recasts the question of the relationship between text and interpretation. The text, it seems, is not as original and interpretation appears to be more originary than commonly is assumed. Text and interpretation are interwoven to form a *textus* which, as Barthes insists, "*is experienced only in an activity, a* production."[18] From this perspective, a text is not a finished product, but is an ongoing production which continuously emerges in and through the activity of interpretation. This play merits further consideration.

The text to be interpreted is, as we have seen, "that ambiguous gift, food, host in the sense of victim, sacrifice. It is broken, divided, passed around, consumed by the critics canny and uncanny who are in that odd relation to one another of host and parasite."[19] The victim, however, is alluring. The text coyly calls to the fertile imagination of the transgressor. If the text is not to lie fallow but is to be impregnated, it must be penetrated, ruptured, victimized.

As Jeffrey Mehlman maintains, "in order to be preserved the text must be interpreted, opened up, violated."[20] Dismembering is, paradoxically, a condition of remembering, death the genesis of life. This drama can unfold only on a stage where "murder is endless and is repeated indefinitely,"[21] a stage where there is no curtain to fall.

Having recognized the way in which the parasite which feeds on the host nourishes its victim, we are in a position to see that incorporation is not mere destruction but is also reembodiment, reincarnation. Consequently, the sacrifice enacted by the transgressor is simultaneously the self-sacrifice of the victim. Following Foucault, "Writing is now linked to sacrifice and to the sacrifice of life itself; it is a voluntary obliteration of self."[22] Through a dialectical inversion, this self-sacrifice becomes self-realization. By creating the possibility of interpretation, the text invites transgression. If confusion is to be avoided, it is essential to stress that interpretation is not extrinsic to the text, but is intrinsic to the text's own becoming. There is no text-in-itself which subsists apart from interpretation. Since interpretation is intrinsic to text, interpretation is not secondary to a more primary original, but is always an interpretation of that which itself is already an interpretation. Every text is a labyrinthine chain of interpenetrating interpretations, or, to use Kierkegaard's image, is a "Chinese puzzle box." There is no more *a* (T)text than there is *an* (A)author. No text, in other words, is author-itative and no author is origin-al. The infinite play of interpretation in which writing and reading are *both* the interpretation of interpretation establishes the ineradicable textuality of the text. As Kierkegaard intimates and Barthes contends, the text is "play, task, production, and activity. This means that the Text requires an attempt to abolish (or at least to lessen) the distance between writing and reading, not by intensifying the reader's projection into the work, but by linking the two together in a single signifying process [*pratique signifiante*]."[23]

The host, we are forced to conclude, is a parasite on a

parasite, thereby constituting the parasite a host. The parasite-become-host, of course, itself harbors a parasite, i.e., the host-become-parasite. By offering itself as a sacrifice, the text infects interpretation, wounds the transgressor from within. The struggle to settle the unsettled unsettles and the effort to familiarize the strange estranges. The inwardization of the outward turns everything inside-out. R. D. Laing explores this "nomad thought."

> One is inside
> then outside what one has been inside,
> One feels empty
> because there is nothing inside oneself
> One tries to get inside oneself
>   that inside of the outside
>   that one was once inside
>   once one tries to get onself inside what
>   one is outside. . .[24]

The transgressor discovers the nerve of failure to be the failure of success. Since host and parasite are inseparable, to eat is always also to be eaten—to be consumed from within by a host (*hostia*) transformed into a Ghost (*Ghosti*).[25] The devoured text returns to haunt the transgressor like a dead, slain, absent father. "The critical text and the literary text," according to Miller, "are each parasite and host for the other, each feeding on the other and feeding it, destroying and being destroyed by it."[26]

Appearances to the contrary notwithstanding, this mutual consumption is creative. Not only creative, but actually salutary, for as Brown insists, "Eating is redemptive."[27] Perhaps this is Foucault's point when he writes: "Transgression opens onto a scintillating and constantly affirmed world, a world without shadow or twilight, without that serpentine 'no' that bites into fruits and lodges their contradictions at their core. It is the solar inversion of satanic denial. It was originally linked to the divine, or rather, from this limit marked by the sacred it opens the space where the divine functions."[28] Transgression, however, reveals the divine only by violating, rupturing, breaking all we have deemed holy. "Finally," asks Nietzsche, "what remained to be sacrificed? At long last, did one not have to sacrifice for once whatever is comforting, holy, healing; all hope, all faith in hidden harmony, in future blisses and justices? Didn't one have to sacrifice God himself and, from cruelty against oneself, worship the stone, stupidity, gravity, fate, the nothing? To sacrifice God for the nothing—this paradoxical mystery of the final cruelty was reserved for the generation that is now coming up."[29] By reenacting this sacrifice in the Theater of Cruelty, transgressors discover that "the divine has been ruined by God. That is to say, by man, who in permitting himself to be separated from Life by God, in permitting himself to be usurped from his own birth, became man by polluting the divinity of the divine."[30]

The interpretation of interpretation as S/Tex(t)ual transgression turns out to be a dangerous game, a game in which there is no room for spectators. Indeed if we follow the *via rupta*, "There is no longer spectator or spectacle, but *festival*. All the limits furrowing classical theatricality (represented/representer, signified/signifier, author/director/actors/spectators, stage/audience, text/interpretation, etc.) were ethico-metaphysical prohibitions, wrinkles, grimaces, rictuses—the symptoms of fear before the dangers of the festival. Within the space of the festival opened by transgression, the distance of representation should no longer be extendable. The festival of cruelty lifts all footlights and protective barriers before the 'absolute danger' which is 'without foundation'."[31] This "dangerous festival" which is the "solar inversion of satanic denial" brings "*fröhliche Wissenschaft*":

> The identity of the sacrificer and the victim: the sacrifice of identity. The last cruel sacrifice is sacrifice of the separateness of the self; self-sacrifice, self-slaughter, self-annihilation. The last cruel sacrifice is the crucifixion of the self.[32]

This crucifixion of self is the death of God which is the resurrection of the Word.

DISSEMINATION OF THE WORD

> But what does it mean to kill God if he does not exist, to kill God *who has never existed?* Perhaps it means to kill God both because he does not exist and to guarantee he will not exist—certainly a cause for laughter: to kill God to liberate life from this existence that limits it, but also to bring it back to those limits that are annulled by this limitless existence—as a sacrifice; to kill God to return him to this nothingness he is and to manifest his existence at the center of a light that blazes like a presence—for the ecstasy; to kill God in order to lose language in a deafening night and because this wound must make him bleed until there springs forth "an immense alleluia lost in the interminable silence"—and this is communication. The death of God does not restore us to a limited positivistic world, but to a world exposed by the experience of its limits, made and unmade by that excess which transgresses it.[33]

If, as Nietzsche anticipates, deconstruction is the hermeneutic of the death of God, then the death of God is the (a)theology of deconstruction. A death of God (a)theology, however, really is a *radical* Christology. With Incarnation,

> . . . the theatre was changed
> To something else.[34]

Exploring Artaud's Theater of Cruelty, Derrida explains, "The stage is theological for as long as it is dominated by speech, by a will to speech, by the layout of a primary logos which does not belong to the theatrical site and governs it from a distance." The death of God is the sacrifice of the "author-creator who, absent and from afar, is armed with a text and keeps watch over, assembles, regulates the time or the meaning of representation, letting this latter *represent* him as concerns what is called the content of his thoughts, his intentions, his ideas."[35] Incarnation *irrevocably* erases the disembodied Logos and inscribes a Word which becomes the script enacted in the infinite play of interpretation. When Incarnation is understood as Inscription, we discover Word. Embodied Word is Script(ure), the writing in which we are inscribed and which we inscribe. Thus by viewing Incarnation as Inscription, "we have discerned writing: a nonsymmetrical division designated on the one hand the closure of the book, and on the other the opening of the text. On the one hand the theological encyclopedia and, modeled upon it, the book of man. On the other a fabric of traces marking the disappearance of an exceeded God or of an erased man. The question of writing could be opened only if the book was closed. The joyous wandering of the *graphein* then became wandering without return. The opening into the text was adventure, expenditure without reserve."[36]

The Word inscribes the *via rupta*. Like all writing, the Word transgresses. Incarnation is the embodiment of a struggle of Son against Father which culminates in the violence of parricide.[37] This contest reveals the paradoxical interplay of parricide and suicide, sacrifice and self-sacrifice. Sacrifice of Author through inscription in Word (or text) is self-negation which is self-realization. "All killing," Brown stresses, "is sacrificial, and all sacrifice is eating. Killing is eating."[38] But eating, we have observed, is the act of inwardization, incorporation, embodiment which establishes the sameness of difference. Dismemberment engenders remembering, as the victim is incarnate in the victimizer. The devoured, dead, slain Father returns to haunt the Son like a ghost (a ghost soon acknowledged holy). The presence of the sacrificial victim, in other words, is enacted as absence. Through Inscription, "presence becomes absence, and becomes actual as absence, and that absence is the self-enactment of presence. Therefore, presence can now be actual only in its absence, in its absence from itself, from its own self-identity. But that absence is both a real absence and a real act. Not only is it a real act, it is an act realizing all act, and it realizes all act in this act. Consequently, all self-identity is realized in this act: 'The door is I'."[39] But this door can be opened only through further transgression. This "opening [space/spacing, emptying/*kenosis*] is a closing of all presence."[40] The Word is the closure of presence which is not at the same time absence, the end of identity which is not at the same time difference. As the interplay of presence and absence and of identity and difference, the Word itself can appear only by disappearing. The *Logos Spermatikos* is propagated by dispersal, diffusion, scattering, spreading, sowing—by *dissemination.*

The dissemination of the Word is its reincorporation, reincarnation, or reinscription. In the absence of any text-in-itself, Scripture is always a writing which is a rewriting and a rewriting which must itself be rewritten. This "writing," Geoffrey Hartman reminds us, "is always theft or bricolage of the logos. The theft redistributes the logos by a new principle of equity, as unreferable to laws of property, boundary, etc. (Roman, capitalistic, paternal, national) as the volatile seed of flowers. Property, even in the form of the *nom propre,* is *non-propre,* and writing is an act of crossing [i.e., of transgressing] the line of the text, of making it indeterminate, or of revealing the *midi* as the *mi-dit.* 'La force rare du texte, c'est que vous ne puissiez pas le surprendre (et donc limiter) à dire: *ceci est cela'* (*Glas,* p. 222)."[41] *Ceci est cela,* two become one—the fruit of the dissemination of the Word.

When two become one, we see the sameness of transgressor and transgressed. Having displaced the Lord of Hosts, Word becomes Host. The Word, itself a transgressor, is also a victim who invites transgression. The apparently parricidic act of transgression manifests the host-ility of the Word. Parasite is host, sacrificer a sacrifice. The Word is a hospitable host who not only asks us to sit down at his table, but even offers *himself* for our nourishment: "Take this and eat; it is my body." The Eucharist reveals the Word as "that ambiguous gift, food, host in the sense of victim, sacrifice. It is broken, divided, passed around, consumed."[42] In this communion, the suicide of the Father and parricide of the Son become the fratricide of the brothers. As we have come to suspect, this act of negation is also creative.

Sacrificial appropriation is, of course, a transgression which turns against itself by reincarnating the Word it victimizes. The Word becomes *la parole soufflée*[43] which inspires (*souffler*). This in-spiration is haunting, for Host (*Hostia*)returns as Ghost (*Ghostia*). The dissemination of the Word establishes the identity of sacrificer and sacrifice, victimizer and victim. In the act of transgression, the communicant discovers not only parricide, but also fratricide to be suicide.[44]

If sacrifice and sacrificer are one, then victimizer is also victim. A death of God (a)theology, which is really a radical Christology, finds its completion in the crucifixion of the individual self and the resurrection of universal humanity. This end (or beginning) is realized through the dissemination of the Word. Thomas Altizer correctly maintains that "when the eternal death of Jesus is incorporated into the body of humanity, and incorporated by a form of faith revolving about a continual dying with Christ, then the original descent into Hell can gradually and progressively be actualized in the universal body of humanity. Then the individual and eternal death of Jesus is comprehensively and universally realized in the dissolution of the center or ground of all forms of autonomous and individual self-consciousness. For the actual and real dissolution or death of the center of consciousness brings about the end of all autonomous self-consciousness. Yet the dissolution of self-consciousness is simultaneously the end of all truly individual selfhood, the end of the autonomous ego or the self which is only itself."[45]

The death of God is the birth of the Word (and, of course, vice versa). This erasure of the "transcendental signified" sets the stage for the infinite play of interpretation. In the absence of any (A)author-itative

(S)script-ure, "the place we inhabit, wherever we are, is always this in-between zone, place of host and parasite, neither inside nor outside. It is a region of the *Unheimlich,* beyond any formalism, which reforms itself wherever we are, if we know where we are. This 'place' is where we are, in whatever text, in the most inclusive sense of that word, we happen to be living."[46] Caught in the endless web of textuality, actors lose themselves in the infinity of the play. The dissemination of the Word, Hartman following Derrida, has suggested, "redistributes the logos by a new principle of equity, as unreferable to laws of property, boundary, etc. . . . Property, even in the form of the *nom propre,* is *non-propre.*"[47] Thought, in other words, becomes nomad/no-man thought which no longer is (A)author-ized. This "last cruel sacrifice is the crucifixion of the self."

The vertigo brought by interpretation can be unsettling, even estranging. The absent origin often engenders nostalgia; the lost center frequently breeds despair. But the other side of this Nay is a Yea which is "the solar inversion of satanic denial." As Derrida explains, such Yea-saying is "the joyous affirmation of the play of the world and of the innocence of becoming, the affirmation of a world of signs without fault, without truth, and without origin which is offered to an active interpretation. *This affirmation then determines the noncenter otherwise than as a loss of the center.* And it plays without security. For there is a *sure* play: that which is limited to the *substitution* of *given* and *existing, present,* pieces. In absolute chance, affirmation also surrenders itself to *genetic* indetermination, to the *seminal* adventure of the trace."[48]

"The *seminal* adventure of the trace," is "the joyous wandering of the *graphein.*" This inscription is the dissemination of the Word. "The deconstructive procedure," Miller avers, "by reversing the relation of ghost and host, by playing on the play with language, may go beyond the repetitive generation of nihilism by metaphysics and of metaphysics by nihilism. It may reach something like that *fröhliche Wissenschaft* for which Nietzsche called. This would be interpretation as joyful wisdom, the greatest joy in the midst of the greatest suffering, an inhabitation of that gaiety of language which is our seigneur."[49] If we join this "Bacchanalian revel in which no member is sober,"[50] we discover a "Dionysian Christianity . . . in which meaning is not fixed, but ever new and ever changing."[51] We must never forget, however, that the frenzy of Dionysus is born of "the labor of the negative."[52] "In the Wine presses" of Luvah which, Blake tells us, crush Urizen, "in the Wine presses is wailing, terror and despair."[53] The Dionysian play which makes us all players can be staged only in the Theater of Cruelty where vitalization is victimization and victimization is that festival which "lifts all footlights and protective barriers before the 'absolute danger' which is 'without foundation'." *Le souffleur* prompts authors and readers who play on this stage (*our* stage) to enact a Kierkegaardian "double movement" which paradoxically joins negation and affirmation. Participation in this drama reveals not only the Nay in the Yea, but also the Yea in the Nay. Though there is no exit from the labyrinth which stretches above "70,000 fathoms," the recognition that "the fire and the rose are one"[54] brings "the greatest joy in the midst of the greatest suffering."

NOTES

1. Søren Kierkegaard, *Either-Or,* trans. David F. and Lillian Marvin Swenson (Princeton: Princeton University Press, 1971), vol. 1, p. 7.

2. *Either-Or,* p. 13.

3. *Either-Or,* p. 9.

4. Michel Foucault, "What is an Author?" in *Language, Counter-Memory, Practice,* trans. Donald F. Bouchard (Ithaca: Cornell University Press, 1977), p. 117.

5. Roland Barthes, "From Work to Text," in *Textual Strategies: Perspectives in Post-Structuralist Criticism,* ed. Josué V. Harari (Ithaca: Cornell University Press, 1979), p. 77.

6. Barthes, p. 76.

7. Søren Kierkegaard, *Concluding Unscientific Postscript,* trans. David. F. Swenson and Walter Lowrie (Princeton: Princeton University Press, 1968), p. 551.

8. Jacques Derrida, "La parole Soufflée," in *Writing and Difference,* trans. Alan Bass (Chicago: University of Chicago Press, 1979), p. 176.

9. "What is an Author?" in *Language, Counter-Memory, Practice,* p. 117.

10. Jacques Derrida, *Of Grammatology,* trans. Gayatri Chakravorty Spivak (Baltimore: Johns Hopkins University Press, 1976), pp. 107–8.

11. This is Deleuze's term. See Gilles Deleuze, "Nomad Thought," in *The New Nietzsche: Contemporary Styles of Interpretation,* ed. David B. Allison (New York: Dell Publishing Co., 1977), pp. 142–49.

12. R. D. Laing, *Knots* (New York: Random House, 1970), p. 83.

13. I borrow this phrase from H. Ganse Little.

14. "A Preface to Transgression," in *Language, Counter-Memory, Practice,* p. 34.

15. Norman O. Brown, *Love's Body* (New York: Random House, 1968), p. 165.

16. Brown, p. 165.

17. J. Hillis Miller, "The Critic as Host," in *Deconstruction and Criticism* (New York: Seabury Press, 1978), p. 219.

18. Barthes, p. 75.

19. Miller, p. 225.

20. Jeffrey Mehlman, "The 'Floating Signifier': From Lévi-Strauss to Lacan," *French Freud: Structural Studies in PsychoAnalysis, Yale French Studies,* no. 48, 1972, p. 34.

21. "The Theater of Cruelty," in *Writing and Difference,* p. 249.

22. "What is an Author?" in *Language, Counter-Memory, Practice,* p. 117. See above, n. 9.

23. Barthes, p. 79.

24. Laing, p. 83.

25. Miller, pp. 220–21.

26. Miller, p. 249.

27. Brown, p. 167.

28. "A Preface to Transgression," in *Language, Counter-Memory, Practice,* p. 37.

29. Nietzsche, *Beyond Good and Evil*, trans. Walter Kaufmann (New York: Random House, 1966), p. 67.

30. "The Theater of Cruelty," in *Writing and Difference*, p. 243.

31. "The Theater of Cruelty", p. 244.

32. Brown, p. 171.

33. "A Preface to Transgression," in *Language, Counter-Memory, Practice*, p. 32. Cf. J. Hillis Miller, *The Disappearance of God: Five Nineteenth-Century Writers* (Cambridge: Harvard University Press, 1963).

34. Wallace Stevens, "Of Modern Poetry," *The Collected Poems of Wallace Stevens* (New York: Knopf, 1972), pp. 239–40.

35. "The Theater of Cruelty," in *Writing and Difference*, p. 235.

36. "Ellipsis," in *Writing and Difference*, p. 294.

37. Consider, for example, Freud's comment: "The very deed in which the son offered the greatest possible atonement to the father brought him at the same time to the attainment of his wishes *against* the father. He himself became God, beside, or, more correctly, in the place of, the father. A son-religion displaced the father-religion. As a sign of this substitution the ancient totem meal was derived in the form of communion, in which the company of brothers consumed the flesh and blood of the son—no longer the father—obtained sanctity thereby and identified themselves with him. Thus we can trace through the ages the identity of the totem meal with animal sacrifice, with the anthropic human sacrifice and with the Christian Eucharist, and we can recognize in all these rituals the effect of the crime by which men were so deeply weighed down but of which they must nonetheless feel so proud. The Christian communion, however, is essentially a fresh elimination of the father, a repetition of the guilty deed." *Totem and Taboo*, trans. James Strachey (New York: W. W. Norton and Co., 1950), pp. 154–55. This insight is central to the theory of literary criticism developed by Harold Bloom. See, *inter alia*, *The Anxiety of Influence: A Theory of Poetry* (New York: Oxford University Press, 1973). Cf. Foucault's "The Father's 'No'," in *Language, Counter-Memory, Practice*, pp. 68–86.

38. Brown, p. 164.

39. Thomas J. J. Altizer, *The Self-Embodiment of God* (New York: Harper & Row, 1977), p. 88.

40. Altizer, p. 88.

41. Geoffrey H. Hartman, *Criticism in the Wilderness: The Study of Literature Today* (New Haven: Yale University Press, 1980), p. 205.

42. Miller, p. 225. See above, n. 19.

43. See "La parole soufflée," in *Writing and Difference,* pp. 169–95.

44. Or as Brown puts it: "Murder is misdirected suicide, to destroy part of oneself; murder is suicide with mistaken identity" (p. 162).

45. Thomas J. J. Altizer, *The Descent into Hell: A Study of the Radical Reversal of the Christian Consciousness* (New York: Seabury Press, 1979), p. 154.

46. Miller, p. 231.

47. Hartman, p. 205. See above, note 41.

48. "Structure, Sign, and Play," in *Writing and Difference,* p. 292.

49. Miller, pp. 230–31.

50. Hegel, *Phenomenology of Spirit,* trans. by A. V. Miller (New York: Oxford University Press, 1977), p. 27.

51. Brown, p. 196.

52. Hegel, p. 10.

53. William Blake, *The Four Zoas,* IX, 732.

54. T. S. Eliot, *Little Gidding.*

4

ROBERT P. SCHARLEMANN

The Being of God
When God Is Not Being God
Deconstructing the History of Theism

*Horruit creatura stupescens ac dicens: quidnam est hoc novum
mysterium? Iudex iudicatur et quietus est; invisibilis videtur
neque erubescit; incomprehensibilis prehenditur neque indigna-
tur; incommensurabilis mensuratur neque repugnat; impassibilis
patitur neque ulciscitur; immortalis moritur neque respondet
verbum.*

MELITO OF SARDIS, *Fragm. 13*

I

In his lectures on Augustine and then, later, in his *Being and
Time* (1927), Martin Heidegger undertook what he called a
"destruction" (*Destruktion*) of the history of ontology, with
the stated aim of retrieving the question of the meaning of
being, which has been lost, or forgotten, in the metaphysical tradition. After him, there were some sporadic attempts
to "destrue" (if one may coin a word parallel to "construe")—to destructure, or to deconstruct—the history of
theism in a similar fashion. Dietrich Bonhoeffer's disserta-
tion, entitled *Akt und Sein*,[1] was discernibly influenced by
the early Heidegger and is one of the first indications of
how the attempt might be made; but one can also understand the later Bonhoeffer's concern with secularity, together with his rejection of a metaphysical and religious

79

deity, as indicating the same intention. Still, nothing has been done, with the theistic tradition, on the same daunting scale as Heidegger's continual rereadings, by taking apart and putting together again, of the history of ontology in the West. It has been argued that the theological counterpart of Heidegger in this respect may have been none other than Karl Barth, despite his own, "Barthian" reputation. It is not difficult to find the texts in Barth to support such an argument. Indeed, that Barth was never a theist in the traditional sense still seems clear; for, like Heidegger on the meaning of being, he placed the actuality of God prior to the logical form of contradiction. This is an aspect of Barth obscured by much of his own work, as well as by his more biblicistic followers. But it is unmistakable, among other places, in the famous controversy with Emil Brunner over whether there can be a natural theology and whether there is a point of contact in human being for the revelation of God. For, among the reasons behind the sharp *Nein*! of his reply, with its "angry introduction," as he titled it, lay his warning that a concern with natural theology would inevitably reintroduce the division between believers and unbelievers, theists and atheists, that has caused mischief in theology for so many centuries. The new theology must reach back, instead, to a place anterior to such divisions, in order to start with the reality of a revelation that is unaffected by the differences between belief and unbelief, theism and atheism, being and nonbeing, optimism and pessimism, and all the rest. Amidst all this, however, Barth seemed never entirely willing to follow his own lead, as if the weight of Protestant biblicism was too much for him to cast off completely. In the end, his theology remained a mixture of an old theism with a new, "destructive" reading of the history of theism in the way it interpreted the theological tradition. The symptom of this is that Barth, like theistic thought otherwise, left the concept of the being as such unthought while he directed his attention to the being *of* God or *of* the creature. Nothing shows this, *in nuce*, more clearly than his reconstruction of the being of God brought into view by the paradoxes—"the immortal dies and does not say a word in response"—formulated in the fragment from Melito of Sardis quoted at the head of this article.[2] Hence, the task of "destruing" the history of theism has remained, on the whole, unaccomplished.

Obviously, the present essay will not change that state of things. But, with the perspective of the intervening decades and with the advantage offered by the light of the many variations on the theme of destruction, one can perhaps see more clearly where the task lies.[3]

II

The regressive analysis that is called destruction, when it is applied to the history of thought, whether ontological or theological, is not something purely negative. To destroy, or destrue, is not the same as to do away with; it is, rather, to analyze the elements of the structure of thought and trace them back to their beginning—what that means needs still to be clarified[4]—in order to discover the experience that is at the basis of the structure. In *Being and Time*, section 6, which is entitled "The Task of a Destruction of the History of Ontology," Heidegger gave this account:

> We understand this task [of loosening the hardened tradition and of dissolving its obscurities in order to make the question transparent in its own history] as that of the *destruction* of the traditional standing (*Bestand*) of ancient ontology, a destruction which is carried out *under the guidance of the question of being* and which works toward the original experiences in which the first and thenceforth the leading definitions or determinations of being were achieved.[5]

This amounts to a kind of genealogy, as Heidegger indicated when he called it an "investigative issuing of a birth certificate"; and, more specifically, it is a genealogy of the ontological concept of temporality as the meaning of the being of human existence (*Dasein*). Out of what does this concept spring, of what "parents" was it born? Only by carrying out such a destruction of the tradition does the question of being become an actual question again; only such a destruction provides the proof that the question of the meaning of being is unavoidable and demonstrates what it means to "repeat" this question (p. 26).

From this description of the task, as Heidegger saw it, it is clear why the work of destruction is needed—it is the means for getting behind the self-evidentness of the tradition, behind the practice of taking its concepts as given. Because human being is itself historical—we always are what, in the past, we or someone else already have been—a tradition, as incorporating the past that is we, is capable of taking the self-responsibility that properly belongs to Dasein away from it. Traditional formulations then guide the way questions are put and offer the various standpoints of philosophizing as fixed "types" of question and answer, without ever freeing or obliging one to put the question of the meaning of being on one's own and as a question of one's own. This is how the obscuring, or the forgetting, takes place. For, without repeating the question as one's own, there cannot be any positive recourse to the past in the sense of a productive appropriation of it. That is to say, the traditional formulations not only pass on an understanding of the meaning of being; they also hide it by displacing the questioner through letting the tradition be a substitute for the questioner's own self. Originally, the question of the meaning of being can be asked only in the first person singular—only "I" can ask it on "my" own. But one should not misunderstand this as implying an ultimate individualism—as though only the particular person that I am is affected by the question or concerned with its meaning. Instead, it implies that the very universality of being is appropriable not in the form of something common or general but in the form of the singular;[6] inevitably, everyone asks the question of the meaning of being, but everyone must ask it as an "I." A tradition of concepts can hide this universality because it offers the opportunity of reducing everything to a repetition of pregiven types—

there are Platonists, Aristotelians, and so on—and of avoiding the question by saying it depends on whether one is Platonic or Aristotelian or Hegelian or one of the many other types.

This singularity lies in the nature of the question and of human being as Dasein. The question of the meaning of being is ontological, that is, it is both a form of being and also an act of thinking. In asking it, one not only is directed toward "being" but is also carrying out the being that one is—one is be-ing as one asks about being. The answer to the question, similarly, involves ontological concepts, if "ontological" is taken to designate a concept that contains a self-understanding, a concept that, of itself, simultaneously defines being (as what one is) and also establishes a relation to being (as what one is thinking or asking about). That is to say, an understanding of the self (e.g., to understand that "I" am "here") is simultaneously to exist in a certain way ("for me to be means to be in a world") and to relate oneself to being as the object of one's intention (through the thought of what being means). This is to say that the characteristic defining human being is just this, that Dasein *is* ontological—it is a thinking that is a being, and a being that is a thinking.

If the tradition not only transmits but also hides the question of the meaning of being—since we can treat the ontological concepts as things, without being concerned with what they are concepts of—and if it takes the place of the self that asks the question (since we can treat the types of thought as pregiven forms for selfhood, into one or another of which we must fit, like it or not), then it is important to identify the structure of the traditional concepts in order to uncover what is behind them or what they are about. As it happens, the metaphysical tradition that begins with Greek philosophy is one that understands being on the basis of the world; concepts to grasp being are formed from thoughts of things in the world. There is a symptom of this already in the Greek definition of being as *parousia* ("being present, being before one's eyes"). To be is to be present, so that presence determines both the time and the place of being; being is before our eyes, and it is now. To get at the original experience of being that these definitions formulate, their structure must be taken apart; they must be destrued, in a reversal of the process by which being was first construed as *parousia*.

Here it becomes clear why, despite the connotations of the word *destruction*, this regressive analysis is not intended to wipe out the tradition but to recall what it was about. It is a kind of unraveling, which aims to follow the thread back to the experience of being from which the texture of concepts comes. Destruing the tradition means finding the rule according to which the concepts were formed out of the experience, so that the motion of their genesis can be run backwards. Just as a "constructive definition" (of the kind employed for geometric figures) provides a rule according to which the defined object can be *produced* ("a circle is a line drawn so that the points of the line are equidistant from a single point, a center, which is not part of the line"), so a destructive interpretation or analysis provides a rule for reducing what has been produced, taking the ontological concepts back to the experience of being they formulate and doing so by finding the rule according to which they have been formed. Heidegger's work in *Sein und Zeit* and in the studies that followed it is an illustration of how this can be done. His guideline is the question of how time and being are put together in the history of ontology, if temporality is understood as the meaning of the being of Dasein—if to exist, to be there, means to be timed. The first step back takes us to Kant, specifically to the "schematism" of ideas[7] in the *Critique of Pure Reason* and to his concept of subjectivity. From there one is led still farther back to Descartes, whose notion of subjectivity and time Kant assumed and then formulated precisely. At this second station back, Heidegger works out the unexpressed ontological foundations of the *cogito sum*, showing that Descartes failed to provide an adequate concept for his new beginning in philosophy because he took over the medieval ontology. The self-evident connection that he made between "I think, I am" and "I am *a thinking thing*" is the connection between his new point of departure—an understanding of being based not, as the Greek, on the objectivity of worldly being but upon subjectivity—and the inherited metaphysical concepts; the concepts turn a perception of how "I" am at all into a definition of what a human entity is, in contrast to other entities, namely, a thinking entity. But the significance of this formulation, which shifts categories in the move from "I am, thinking" to "What I am is a thinking thing," can be measured only by going back from the medieval metaphysical concepts to the ontology of ancient Greece, from which they are drawn. The Greek understanding represents, then, the final station along the way back.

How we recognize what is the last station, Heidegger does not explain. But the explanation is not hard to find. Greek thought is the place at which the language of everyday *understanding* is used, for the first time, for the conceptual *definition* of being. This is one way of explaining why the backward steps of Heidegger's destruction retreat to Greek ontology but no farther. For destruction takes the tradition back to earlier concepts—to Kant to Descartes to the Scholastics and then to Aristotle and Plato—until it reaches the point where the concepts are first formed as concepts, that is, when everyday words which, until that time, expressed an understanding of being and directly showed the world in its light, were enlisted in order to interpret and define the being so understood and shown. Their function of showing the world as it is understood is disrupted by the need to ask what they mean, a disruption that is illustrated when, e.g., "The sky is blue" (to take an example from *Being and Time*) no longer simply shows the sky in a certain way, or says how the sky is, but prompts the question "What does 'is' mean? What does it mean that the sky 'is' blue?" Ontological concepts come into being when the words which normally say that things are something, and how and what they are, themselves become objects of attention—"is" not only says the sky in its blueness but itself becomes an object of attention.

Greek ontology did understand being on the basis of time, and specifically, it understood the meaning of being as that of being present. Nevertheless, because it used concepts designating things in the world in order to characterize the being so understood, this ontology *conceived* of time not as the basis of being or as the meaning of being but as another entity, a thing in the world; time was something. This, we might say, is Heidegger's basic rule for destruing the metaphysical concepts—they contain an understanding of being, and of temporality as the meaning of human being, but they formulate that understanding in concepts that make of being and the meaning of being an entity among other entities. In these concepts, being and time appear as entities that, nonetheless, are not entities; they involve a contradiction in the concepts defining them because the difference between time and other entities, like the difference between being as such and entities, remained unthought.

To the first rule of destruction a second can be added; namely, that the structures of being were worked out in Greek ontology according to the way in which being appeared in talk (*legein*). In popular as well as philosophical Greek understanding, Dasein was understood as the *zoon logon echon,* "the living thing that can talk." Hence, the capacity for *legein* became the guideline for articulating the structure of being. At first, this led to Plato's dialectic; but as the hermeneutics of logos progressed, an ever more radical version of the problem became possible, so that, in Aristotle, not dialectic, but talking (*legein*) or even *noein* ("thinking," in the sense of the simple perceiving of what is there at hand) became the guideline. And since talking has the temporal structure of presenting something—when one talks about something, one presents it to mind—the being of entities is conceived of as presence: real entities are those that are perceptibly there, in front of our senses, especially our seeing, or of our mind, now.

It is not only in Greek thought, however, that there is a close connection of language—"language" in the sense that German, French, and English are languages but symbolic logic and computer codes are not[8]—with the being of human beings; for, like Dasein, a word is itself ontological; it is a perceptible thing that is also a meaning and a meaning that is also a perceptible thing. If the being of Dasein is care, or concern (*Sorge*), then the being of language is sign. Ontologically, language and Dasein are mirrors for each other: we can see what our acts of thinking-being are by their expression in language, and we can understand language by an awareness of our acts of thinking being. Dasein is a thinking that is a being, as language is a thing that is a thought.

III

Does the destruction of the history of ontology, as Heidegger envisaged it in *Being and Time,* involve any theological issues? In a way, of course, it must, since the history of ontology and the history of theology are intimate partners in Western thought. But we are looking, more specifically, for that formation in theology which, like the conception of being as being present, calls for an analysis of how it came to have the structure it has and which, in its traditional standing, hides what it originally signified. The elements in the work of destruction are, as the preceding section indicated: (1) that destruction reverses the construction, for it takes apart what has been put together in the history of thought; (2) that this dismantling serves the aim of regaining access to the experience that is at its basis by finding the rule of production of the concepts; and (3) that the original experience—whether that of being or of God or of the unity of the two—exceeds what can be grasped in everyday or cosmic concepts. By retrieving the original experience, one may be able to reformulate it in concepts that are more adequate to the experience itself than are the traditional ones.

For Heidegger, as he viewed the history of ontology, the basis lay in a revelation of being. That this revelation has been covered over by the metaphysical concepts, and the sciences derivative from them, is shown by how the question of the meaning of being has been forgotten. For theology, we can ask whether, corresponding to the oblivion of the meaning of being, there is a forgetfulness of God, not only in the sense that Schleiermacher gave the term in section 11 of his *The Christian Faith,* which describes the human condition as one of God-forgetfulness rather than of the denial of God, but, more specifically, as forgetting the *otherness* of God. The thesis I should like to propound here is that, in the theological tradition, the otherness of God (the being of God when God is not being God, or the freedom of God both to be and not to be) has remained unthought and conceptually forgotten in exactly the same manner as has the question of the meaning of being. The symbol of the otherness of God (incarnate deity, or existent deity) is subject to the same oblivion in the history of theology as the question of the meaning of being is in the metaphysical tradition. Not God and not being are what is forgotten, but the *question of the meaning* of being and the *symbol of the otherness* of God. Hence, just as the symptom of the forgottenness of the meaning of being lies in our regarding the question "What does it mean for X to be what it is?" as nonsensical, so the symptom of the forgottenness of the otherness of God lies in our regarding as unintelligible the symbol of God (existent deity) which is the being of God when God is not being God.

To forget being, according to Heidegger's understanding, is to forget the question of the meaning of being, both in the sense of asking what the word *being* signifies and also in the sense of disregarding that being is the possibility most one's own. The symptom of such forgetfulness is that, instead of understanding being, we discuss the concept of being, and being is discussed not as something we can do, our own possibility, but as a concept, a view, a position, already given in the tradition to which we belong, or as a transempirical object about which one can hold different, though undecidable, views. Thus, for example, an analysis may distinguish between the singularity and the generality of a thing, or between how it is concretely perceived and how it is abstractly thought, but, in the process, what is left out is just the connection between the singular and the general, the concrete and the abstract, that is expressed by the word *is* and that represents the being of the thing. We distinguish between the formal correctness (validity), similarly, and the truth of an argument, but we leave out of theoretical consideration the actual fusion of the formal with the material in any living thought. How to understand and to interpret just the connection between the formal and the nonformal is left to the vagaries of practice and prudence. As a consequence of forgetting being in this way, it is considered sensible and intelligible to ask what the meaning of a word is, or what someone means by a certain word, but it is considered to be nonsensical or unintelligible, or the result of confusion, to ask what it means for a thing to be the thing it is.

Theologically, this kind of question—what it means for a thing to be the thing it is—is answered, in one way, by the symbol of creation, which expresses that what it means to be an entity at all is to have been created, that is, to be the result of the work of a maker. It also expresses that to be an entity is to be something definite in the midst of the possibility of being other, for there is no necessity or reason about anything's being the thing it is; it could always also not have been anything at all or could be something else than what it actually is. The meaning of the being of anything, as expressed in this symbol, is that being there at all is an embodiment of a "can be" instead of a "must be," or of an actuality against the background of possibility. The meaning of creation is freedom rather than contingency.

But the doctrine of creation, which includes the concept of God as the uncreated being (*ens increatum*) in contrast to the creature as *ens creatum* and which carries with it the picture of "making" something, also leads directly into the theistic picture of God, self, and the world. For, according to the concept of finite being as *ens creatum*—where the idea of creating contains the picture of making—the difference between God and the world is thought of as the difference between one who makes something and the thing that is made, analogous to the difference between a sculptor and the sculpture or a painter and the painting. With this picture, there inevitably comes the accompanying thought that the whole of things is one in which there are two different kinds of entities, the creator and the creature, and that the whole, called "being," comprises both. What cannot be thought, in the tradition of this picture, is that the world is itself a moment in the being of God; what cannot be thought is that the world is the being of God when God is not being deity, or the being of God in the time of not being. To reconstruct the picture of the relation between God and the world, after this destruction of the picture, requires rethinking the division between the uncreated and the created according to the idea of God's being God as God and God's being God as other than God. In effect, this would also take the doctrine of creation into the theological dogma of Trinity, if the trinitarian conceptualization is understood as one in which the very being of God incorporates its own otherness: to be God is both to be deity and to be other than deity. But it also takes time into the being of God, by distinguishing *when* God is not being God.

In the theistic picture, the negative is referred to God, the *un*created entity, only as the otherness of the creature—God is *not* creature. When this is put together with the other two aspects of the metaphysical concept, we have the three conceptions that mark the history of theology: God is being itself, God is supreme being, and God is uncreated being (the creator). "Being itself" is understood without a clear distinction between the two senses of "being in general" and of "supreme being"; and uncreated being is a picture that encompasses both. What

remains unthought, in the background, is being as such, as
we shall see presently.

If to forget being is, in effect, to lose sight of the
difference between being and entities (and the symptom of
it is to think that the question of the meaning of being does
not mean anything), the forgetfulness of God is to overlook
the otherness of God—God's being God by being other
than deity. Forgetting the symbol of the otherness of God
is, in this way, a counterpart to forgetting the question of
the meaning of being. About being, two questions can be
asked: (a) What is this thing? (2) What does it mean for this
thing to be what it is? The second question always implies
that the thing, whatever it is, could also have been other
than what it actually is; being, even as manifest in this
entity, is different from this entity, as the background of
otherness for the entity. Of God, similarly, there are two
symbols: (1) The symbol of God as deity, of that in which
one places unreserved trust, or of that which embodies and
elicits ultimate concern. This symbol of deity is the "I am"
who delivers us from bondage. (2) The symbol of the
otherness of God, which is the "I am" of Jesus in his worldly
end, or of some other singular name in its worldly end. Just
as the question of the meaning of being can be forgotten, so
that we do not ask: "What does it mean for a thing to be
what it is and not something else or not at all?" so too the
symbol of the otherness of deity can be forgotten, so that
we do not see that "I" may be other than the person who
speaks and that God may be other than deity. Forgetting
being shows up in no longer asking what the meaning
of being is; forgetting God shows up in not ascertaining the
God that is other than the "I" of "I am here" (Dasein), or
that the God of "I am here" is God's being God when God
is other than deity. One can confuse being with a supreme
genus or the highest being; one can confuse deity with a
supreme "I," or an unconditional subject.

The same observations can be stated more radically. To
forget being itself is to lose sight of what comprises both

being and not being, both the whole of being and nothing, both identity and difference. Similarly, to forget God is to lose sight of what comprises both the self and the not-self, the depth of the being of selfhood. The "I am here" of Dasein—the being of any human entity—is then not distinguished from the "I am here" of one who is other than the human subject. To symbolize the self in "I am here" as *other* than the speaking person can very easily appear to be as nonsensical as to ask what it means for a tree to be what it is and not something else or nothing. Who can "I" possibly be if not the one speaking or someone like it? Despite what analytical philosophers are wont to say, this question is not the result of confusing words with things, as though, knowing that we can ask about the meaning of words, we fall into the trap of thinking that we can ask about the meaning of beings and of being as well. Instead, to regard the question of the meaning of being as nonsensical or confused is itself attributable to having forgotten the meaning of being, that is, to having forgotten that an entity can signify (carry a meaning or a sense) just as can a word, because an entity not only is what it is but also embodies a possibility of being against a background of being other; it is what it is against the possibility that it might have been other or could become other than what it now is. Similarly, if we consider it self-evident that the "I" of "I am here" is the person of the one speaking—since pronouncing the word "I" is to make oneself an instance of what the word refers to—then to ask who the self of "I am" is, is as nonsensical as asking about the meaning of being; but this is only a symptom of having forgotten the otherness that God is. "Who am I other than the one here, or there, or at another place?" is as pointless as asking "What does it mean for X to be X?" But this is a pointlessness that vanishes when the depth in which both I and not-I have their origin is uncovered or recalled. To forget the otherness, the negation, in God means being oblivious both of the difference that is in the "I" of "I am here"—the difference between Dasein and deity—and also of the difference that is in God and that makes it possible for God to be God as other than deity.

There is, to be sure, an experience of the otherness of God contained in the theistic picture, which is indicated by the placing of God outside the whole world and the human race. But the picture is a picture *of* being as a whole—of the whole of being, in which God, world, and Dasein are three kinds of being. In the theistic conception, which this picture portrays, the concept of being is all-encompassing; there is divine being, human being, and cosmic being, but all are subsumable under the heading of "being." The mode in which they are what they are differs, but "to be" is common to all of them.

One of the major problems arising from this conception is how to think of the relation between finite and infinite being, if finitude belongs to Dasein and world, and infinity is the being of God. This involves two questions, both of which offer a first indication of why being as such remains unthought in the theistic picture: first, the relation of entities to being, and, second, the relation of finite to infinite. Aristotle already rejected the idea that being is the universal genus to which entities and kinds are related as species. A genus is that universal with reference to which species can be both compared and differentiated—the maple and the oak are both trees, but they are different trees. But the generic concept, in turn, can be definite because it is distinguished from other generic concepts by reference to a still more common genus, the ground of the similarity and the difference. The concept of being, however, allows of no such definition because there is nothing with which it can be contrasted. Since it lacks the determination necessary for a generic concept, its relation to entities cannot be that of a genus to species or a species to particulars. Instead, Aristotle spoke of the "analogy" of being. Though the being that appears in all entities cannot be defined, since the condition for definition is missing, it can be understood, or intuited, because of how it appears in all entities.

This line of thought has been incorporated into the theistic picture, since the relation of creatures to the creator can be understood as the relation of entities to being—but only on condition that God is equated with being itself, *Deus est ipsum esse.* What is pictured as the uncreated entity is understood as the entity in which, by analogy, being appears. Every creature participates in the creator in the way that every entity participates in being. As being appears in all entities according to the measure, or "collection" (*ana logian*), of each, God is the creativity that appears, according to measure, in each of the creatures. When used in theology, this doctrine of the analogy of being did not serve, originally, to give intellectual control over deity, as though our knowledge of being could be used to determine what God is and must be. One might read Barth's rejection of the *analogia entis*—which he once called *the* invention of the anti-Christ and the reason, next to which other reasons were shortsighted and frivolous, for not becoming Catholic[9]—in this fashion; but, as Eberhard Jüngel has argued, Barth's objection was based not on the idea that the analogy of being makes God accessible but on the way it makes one overlook the nearness of God.[10] The doctrine of the analogy of being arises out of a motive different from that of finding a criterion for judging deity; it arises not from the motive of the fullness and definiteness of our knowledge of being through its appearances in entities but from the indefiniteness that results from the inability, in principal, to define and delimit or demonstrate the concept of being as we can other concepts. What is known by analogy remains undefinable and ungraspable.

The point at which this doctrine calls for destruction is not, then, its purported claim to control what deity can and cannot be but, instead, the matter in it that remains unthought, namely, the unthought difference between God and being, and between the general and the supreme, which is a part of not thinking of being as such. The difference between the general and the supreme (between overall being and being over all) can also be called the difference

between the one and the one: "one" in the sense of anyone
at all ("one does not do that") and one in the sense of The
One, the supreme and only one, the one next to whom
there is no equal ("I, the Lord your God, am One"). True,
that difference is acknowledged in the idea that God utterly
transcends the creatures. But it is not incorporated into the
theistic conception. This is shown, for example, by the way
the scholastic term "first cause" can mean, indiscriminately,
the "absolute beginning," the first of a series, and the
"causality" that is the quality expressed by all causes, as
being is expressed in all beings, analogously. Similarly, *qui
est* ("one who is") as the name of God is not distinguished
from the same phrase as applicable to anyone who is.
Alongside the identity between God and being, formulated
in the proposition that God is being itself, there is,
accordingly, always the difference, unthought, between the
two. God is not being itself, if for no other reason than that
participation in being is not the same as participation in
deity. Nongodly being is outside God; it is not God, and it
is what God is not.

With this we are brought to the heart of the theistic
problem. If, for the history of ontology, as Heidegger
destrues it, the question is that of being and time, then, for
the history of theism, the question is that of God and the
time of negation. What is the connection of God with time
and with "not"? The theistic picture does not depict the
experience of the time of negation—namely, that worldly
being (the being of what is not God and what God is not) is
the being of God when God is not being God; it does not
depict the phenomenon of the world as a moment of time in
the being of God. Nor does it contain the difference in the
negative itself, the difference between the negative stated
in the proposition that a subject is not an object (and
conversely) and the negative stated in the proposition that
the infinite is not the finite. In the speculative idealism of
the nineteenth century, this difference—between negation
and the negation of negation—became the focus of the
dialectical concept of God. What Hegel distinguished as the

bad infinite, which is the endlessness or interminability of
something, from the good infinite, which is the "reconciliation" of the opposites constituting finitude, introduces the
thought of that difference into the concept of the infinite.
For, if one thinks of the infinite as the nondialectical opposite of the finite, then it is limited by the finite, as the
positive is limited by the negative, the subjective by the
objective, and so on; but if the infinite is limited, then it is
not infinite; hence, the infinite that is conceived of as the
simple opposite of the finite is not truly infinite but, in its
own turn, finite. This is to say that defining the infinite by
setting it over against the finite is to deny the infinity of the
infinite.

In contrast to this spurious infinite, the dialectical
concept thinks of the infinite as the opposite *of the opposition*
that is the definition of finitude itself. Finitude is
constituted by the limitation of subject upon object, and so
on; each is defined by, and dependent upon, the other to be
what it is. In that sense, finitude is negation—each is what
the other is not. The infinite is the negation of this
negation—it is different from the difference between a
subject and an object or a positive and a negative because it
is both of them. It is the opposite of the opposition, and, in
being that opposite, it is also the unity or reconciliation of
the opposite members.

But even speculative idealism, which did thus distinguish
the difference in negation and see through the illusory
concept of infinite, did not think the difference between
God and the infinite.

These unthought differences become clear when
analyzing Anselm's formulation of the name of God as "that
than which something greater cannot be thought." Even
Barth, however, who made much use of this definition in
laying the foundation of his *Church Dogmatics* and whose
Fides quaerens intellectum ("Faith seeking understanding")
provides one of the most acute and comprehensive analyses
of it, seems to have missed these differences. The otherness
of God is formulated, in Anselm, in a way that connects it

with an existential possibility—God is that than which we "cannot think" a greater. But the incompatibility of this formulation with the theistic picture of God, self, and world in the whole of being is almost immediately obvious. For if being comprises both God and the world, both divine and nondivine being, then there is something greater than God—the whole of being; and to think being is, accordingly, to think what is greater than God. Implicitly, Anselm's definition contains a prohibition against the very metaphysics, the thought of being as being, that he helped to bring into alliance with theology. Would it be too farfetched to conjecture that the voluntarism of the late Middle Ages as well as the antimetaphysical strand in such Protestant dogmatics as those of Schleiermacher and Barth are a reflection of this same connection between the name of God and the prohibition against the thinking of being as such? However that may be, "being," in the theistic picture, comprises both God and what is not God. At least in quantitative terms, therefore, the whole of being is greater than God. There is something outside God, and when one adds that to the thought of God, the sum is more than God alone. Yet, if God is to be understood as that than which a greater thing cannot be thought, then, in the theistic picture, either being is God and God is not truly God or, in anxiety before this prospect, one must desist from thinking being at all, one must forget being in order to save the God of the theistic picture.

Destruing the theistic picture is one way of showing why the deity of the God than whom a greater cannot be thought transgresses the affirmations of theism and embraces atheistic negations as well. It also shows another way of recognizing when the destruction has reached the beginning. Historically, as Heidegger's train to Greek ontology shows, the beginning is found at that point where everyday language, instead of being used to show the world, is used to define the being of what is shown. But, in subject matter, the origin is found at the place where the concepts are self-contradictory—where it appears that the entity time is no entity or that the God of theism is not deity. This is the point at which the concepts are purely open to the reality they are to grasp. The same is so even in the relation between concepts and things in the world. We cannot think the exact appearance of a color, for example, without starting from the thought that X is and is not that color. Subsequently we can determine in what respects X is, and in what respects it is not, the given color. But the condition for being able to make this further determination is the pure openness of mind to reality that is contained in the combination of being and not being, the thought that X is and is not.

Anselm's own interest, of course, lay elsewhere than in the question of the name of that whole which includes God and non-God; it lay, rather, in determining whether the God so named and defined can be merely a thought-entity without also being a real entity. Yet the name that prevents thinking God as only a thought-entity (because what is only a thought-entity cannot be "that than which a greater cannot be thought") also prevents thinking God as part of a whole of being, even as the supreme being in that whole; for as one member of the whole, such a deity is less than the whole. Only if God is being itself, divine as well as nondivine, is this conclusion avoidable; only if God includes a theism as well as an atheism with respect to the theistic picture is God one than whom something greater cannot be thought.

In Anselm, this difference between God and the whole of being remained unthought, as did the difference in the negative, which emerges when we reword the name to say God is that than which "nothing greater" can be thought. For this can mean either: (1) Given X, if X can be thought to be greater, then the one called God is not God, or: (2) Nothing *can* be thought to be greater than God, that is to say, we can think the thought of nothing and, when we do so, we are thinking of what is greater than God, when God is identical with being. In the thought of nothing, we are confronted with what is greater than deity. This second interpretation of "nothing can be thought to be greater" associates freedom with nihilism and order with theism, and it is the thought behind contemporary nihilism. To pose the issue, theologically, as the decision between God and nothing—"Either God or nothing!" "Either theism or nihilism!"—is to miss the God who, even in the time of nothing, is God, the God who is God even when not being deity.

The oblivion, then, that we are speaking of has as its symptoms that we consider to be nonsensical something which makes no sense only because we have forgotten what it is about. Such is the case with the question of the meaning of being ("What does it mean for X to be what it is?") and the symbol of the otherness of God (the symbol "God" as the self that is other than the I of the person speaking the "I am," and the symbol that is existent deity when God is other than deity, both symbols concentrated in the "I am" of Jesus in his worldliness). But this same symptom can appear in the guise of differences that, in the tradition, have not yet been made the object of thought. Such are the differences between the general and the supreme (the thought that the most general is not the same as the highest), between God and being (the thought that God is not identical with being), between nothing and nothing (nothing as no thing and nothing as "not," the sheer otherness of being), and between the negativity of finitude (the self is not the world, and conversely) and infinite negativity (the negation of that negation).

IV

Destruction analyzes the history of thought in order to discover what the thought is about by getting back to its origins, which appear at the point of self-contradiction in the thought. What is the referent of the theistic picture? What is it a picture of? Is it about being as a whole, constituted by the interplay of God, who is only God, and the entities that are not God? This question can be evaded or, again, forgotten; for a picture which, like the theistic picture, shows the meaning of a metaphysical tradition of thought takes on an independent existence once it is formed. Like a photograph, it can be contemplated, retouched, and reproduced without regard to whether it is a picture of anything at all; or it can be treated as a photographic likeness of something that, of itself, is never seen. The picture can become the object, signifying only itself; other pictures can be made of it, but there is nothing of which it is a picture. Indeed, it *can* mean and signify only itself if what it depicts is something that, in principle, can never be seen at all—a view of the whole of things from outside the whole.

But the question of referent takes a turn that should not be disregarded. It is one thing to say that a picture has no referent because it is not a photographic likeness of anything; it is another thing to say that a picture is about something, and therefore has a referent, even though it is not a likeness of anything. The question of referent is not necessarily whether there is something in reality that looks the same as what is described or imagined in a picture. This is evident even in the normal relation between meaning (or sense) and referent. A meaning is what we understand in a word or a sign; and a referent is that to which the meaning points. When we hear the statement "The leaf is green," we may picture what we understand through a mental image of a green leaf. We say the statement has a referent if there is something that is a leaf and is green. In objective terms, we do not make a distinction between the referent as the green leaf and the referent as the being green that the leaf represents; and this is so, in part, because we make no difference generally between the picture of a thing and the picture of the being of that same thing. Even in this everyday case, however, the relation between the words which bear the meaning (the visual or acoustic figure "green leaf") and the mental picture that is formed of the meaning is not one of likeness; for the words do not look anything like the leaf they mean and signify. In principle, the same holds for the relation between the meaning and the referent too. There can be a referent for a meaning even though the meaning does not yield a picture that looks anything like something real. The world about which a poem is written may not look like anything in the physical world, but it is still a referent of the words of the poem.

What, then, is the referent of the theistic picture? Theologically, this question is complicated by the fact that, in the biblical tradition and the theology shaped by it, there is a sense in which the very word *God* is what the word *God* is about. That is to say, there is an identity between God and the word *God,* and between the being of God and the being of language, that is part of the same tradition as that to which the theistic picture belongs. This identity is rooted in the way the word *God* embodies the meaning of any word as a word—its function is to be a sign-of. A word, in contrast to an empty sound, is characterized by its carrying a meaning; it is a sign, a perceptible figure that serves not to call attention to itself but to lead the mind to the meaning it carries. When we understand a language, we do not pay attention to the sound and sight of the words themselves, but we grasp the meaning the words carry. In that sense, every word is a sign, a pointer-to. It points to the meaning it carries, and that meaning, in turn, points to the referent that is signified. So, for example, when we hear the word *tree* (in the context of an intelligible discourse), we understand that the word, though it is different from the object, is *of* the object. This "being of" while "not being" is the structure of a sign (or of what, today, is usually called a "symbol" in theology). It links words with things without eliminating the difference between the two. The reality of the perceptible and intelligible world of everyday depends upon upholding the difference between meaning and referent, between what something says and what it is about; for without the distinction, the reality of the world out there disappears or becomes confused with subjective states.

Theologically, however, the matter is complicated, not

because "God" and theological discourse have no referent, but because there is a sense in which the word *God* refers to the word *word,* and the word *word* refers to the word *God*—so that language is the reality to which the meaning of the word *God* refers and the word *God* is the reality to which the meaning of language points; God *is* what language *means,* and language is what God means. The word, which normally is not the referent but is about the referent is, here, the referent, though without eliminating the difference between the word and the object. I think, if I read him correctly, Karl Daub was the first to point out that the word *God* is the reality to which the sign character of language points, or to which it refers through its meaning as sign-of, and that the phenomenon of language (or the single word *word*) is, in turn, the reality to which the word *God* refers, since the word *God* means sign-of or pointer-to.

In what way does God mean sign-of or pointer-to? It has the sense of "not-I" and "not-this," the one that "I" and "this" are not and that is not "I" or "this." God means the negative that can be instantiated upon any object and any subject by the saying of the word. The word *instantiates* the negation—that is to say, it turns the subject by which it is spoken or the object to which it is applied into a sign of the subject's or object's own otherness. God appears as the otherness that can be at the place where any subject or any object is. Like the words *I, this, here,* and similar ones, the word *God* always has a referent because the very naming of the word creates a referent out of the thing upon which the "not," the intended otherness, is made manifest. In actual talk, one cannot say the word *I* without becoming the one so named, and one cannot say the word *this* without making something the object referred to. Similarly, one cannot say *God* without becoming or indicating the otherness that appears in the negation of the subject or the object or both. *God* refers to the otherness that is manifested upon the speaking subject or the object spoken of or both. In this way, the word *God* refers to the otherness that is manifested upon the speaking subject or the object spoken of or both.

In this way, the word *God* is the reality of God, just as the words *I* and *this* are the realities of the subject and the object. But they are those realities *potentially*—the word *I*, because of the meaning it bears, makes it *possible* for a subject to come to be at all, as the word *this* does for an object. So the word *God* makes it *possible* for a subject or an object to be the sign-reality that is God's presence, the otherness that is there in the naming. This is not the same as saying that the word has no referent outside itself or that it refers only to itself or that there is no difference between the meaning and the referent of the word. But it is to recognize that, unlike the relation between the word *tree* and the object it names, the meaning and the referent are so intimately fused that the meaning makes the referent and the referent appears only with the meaning. Thus, in the theistic picture, it is the *word God* to which the contradiction in the picture refers, and it is this word that makes the picture significant.

To complicate matters still more, the peculiarity of this referential relation in theology is that the referent of the word *God* is given twice over. It is given, first, through what is instantiated with the pronouncing of the word—the subject or object as a sign of what is other than any subject or object and other than the otherness between subjects and objects. And it is given, second, in the phenomenon of language or, by concentration, in the word *word* itself. Thus, there is a double answer to the question of the referent of the word *God.* It refers to the "I" or the "this" upon which, or at which, otherness appears, and it refers to the other word (namely, the word *word*) for the word *God,* or to that as what God is God. "God is God as the word" asserts that "word" (or language) is the way in which God is the deity God is (namely, as not being God, that is, as other than the word *God*). God is God, then, as what is other than God doubly (as the word *word* and also as the word *God*); for the otherness that appears upon a word, which is always a pointer-to, is the same as the otherness as which God exists.

In view of this relation, the question of the extralinguistic referent of theological discourse is, in one sense, not important, since the referent of theological meaning is given in and as language. We do not need to know to what historical and biographical events or to what chemical and physical processes the narrative of Moses and the burning bush—to take this as an example—actually refers, in order to understand what it is about. And we do not need to know to what metaphysical entity the theistic picture refers. But, in another sense, the question of referent is indeed important, and to deny the importance of a certain kind of referent is not the same as saying that the narrative has no referent; for what it is about is not an odd bush or an odd biographical episode, as such, but the otherness that Moses met in the bush. A bush that burns without burning up is certainly "other than" a bush of the world; it "is not" the bush it generically "is." This depiction of the unity of being and not being in the bush is the way in which the narrative speaks of the otherness that is the real referent, an otherness that appears in the theistic picture in the God who is not deity when one thinks being as such.

To destrue the story of the bush does not mean to confine ourselves to such elements of the narrative as the combination of images, the play of sounds and rhythms, and the rhetorical figures instead of ascertaining the referent; it does mean, rather, rediscovering the experience of otherness that is being told in the narrative. What was it that happened to Moses? What would it mean for someone today (for "me") to come face to face with the other voice of "I am"? Or is it the intention of the Mosaic narrative to say that what happened there happened only there and will not happen again? that it can be remembered and recalled but not experienced again, for, having given itself a name, this deity no longer can be encountered in its deity? If so, we cannot ourselves ever expect to encounter the otherness that addressed Moses, but we can understand it, that is to say, we can understand what it was that he heard, even though we cannot hear it for ourselves. It is possible that deity never appears twice in the same way; once the name has been given and heard, it cannot be heard again, though it can be understood, remembered, and recalled. In such a case, God is around only as the absence to which the divine name testifies, though this absence is not like that of what never was and never could be there but like the absence of one who was there and who now has gone for a good reason. Once and only once did the reality appear and leave its name ("I am the one I am"), so that, henceforth, there is no appearance of it except in the name, in every repetition of the words "I am" by anyone. Then it is so that any time anyone thinks or says what is meant by the words "I am" or "I am I" or "I am the one I am," this repetition presents God who, for good reason, has gone. The unity of absence and presence that is intended by this name can be paraphrased, perhaps, by the notion of one who has gone away, for a good reason, in order to return after a while, one whose being away is not to be lamented because the "good reason" is the one named by "freedom." So it is also possible that the God of the theistic picture, who now appears not to be God, is, at the end of the era of theism, the annunciation of a real otherness that can be seen after the Enlightenment.

V

The theistic picture presents the choice of thinking God and forgetting being or of thinking being and denying God because what is in the theistic picture, at its origin, is God who is not being God. To uncover this by a destruction of the picture, however, is to provide the opportunity to think in a different way what cannot be thought there; and that is to think of the relation between God and being by incorporating time and negation into deity. The end of destruction is the beginning of a retrieval of the symbol of existent deity, lost in theism, and of its attendant conception of the being of God when God is not being God. Destruing the theistic picture shows the way in which time and negation remain unthought in the tradition. To think what is unthought is to grasp anew what appears in the picture but is now hidden by the picture itself, and what appears in it at the point of the contradiction sustained by the word *God*—that the theistic God is not deity because something greater can be thought.

In comparing his own reading of the history of thought with that of Hegel, Heidegger drew the following contrast: for Hegel, a conversation with the history of philosophy involved entering into the power and the milieu of what had been thought by earlier thinkers and taking it into one's own thought. For Heidegger, by contrast, the power of earlier thought is not in what past thinkers have already thought but in what they left unthought, the unthought condition of their thinking as they did, from which what they did think gets the room essential for it to be what it is.[11] One could apply a similar description to the destruction of the theistic picture. The intention is guided by the belief that the vitality of theistic thought lies just in what is unthought in the tradition; for God, understood as that than which something greater cannot be thought at all, can be identified with supreme being as long as one does *not* think of being as such but only of infinite or uncreated or divine being in contrast to finite or created or human and cosmic being. In view of the history of metaphysics, Heidegger's program implied that it is possible to carry on traditional metaphysics only as long as one does not think the "ontological difference," the difference between being and entities,[12] that is to say, as long as one does not think the thought that being is *not* any entity. But perhaps—at least, so it seems to me—what is unthought in metaphysics should be stated differently; for the unthought condition of metaphysics is not so much the difference between being and entities as it is the difference between the necessity of thinking that is imposed by the laws of thinking itself, and contained summarily in the law of identity (A is A), and the constraint upon thinking that is effected by how things actually appear to thought. Only as long as one does not think of the difference between that necessity and this constraint is it possible to carry on metaphysics as a working out of those ideas that are necessary to make experience intelligible on the basis of an ideal world behind the appearing world.

But when the unthought gets to be thought, then something must be done besides rethinking the tradition. A deconstruction of the theistic picture, therefore, obliges one to rethink that origin which appears in the picture, as in the metaphysical tradition, at the point where the contradiction is uncovered—the point where, if we think of being as such, then God is not God. I have suggested that the formula for reconstructing that appearance is "the being of God when God is not being God," a formula that includes time and negation in the being of God and that opens thought to deity existing not as a transtemporal or metaphysical entity but as an actuality in life and history.

NOTES

1. Dietrich Bonhoeffer, *Act and Being,* trans. Bernard Noble (New York: Harper & Row, 1961).

2. *Kirchliche Dogmatik,* IV/1, 201–4 (hereafter KD).

3. Whether the abuses of deconstruction can shed light on anything I am not certain. But one can be greatly entertained by a recent report of one such abuse: see Barbara Grizzuti Harrison, "Ah, Nihilism!" *Harper's* 263, no. 1576 (September 1981), 88–93.

4. That "destruction" has not yet attained conceptual clarity is perhaps indicated by there being no entry for *Destruktion* in Braun and Rademacher's lexicon, although there is one for *Konstruktion:* Edmund Braun and Hans Rademacher, *Wissenschaftstheoretisches Lexikon* (Graz, Vienna, Cologne: Verlag Styria, 1978).

5. Martin Heidegger, *Stein und Zeit* (Tübingen: Max Niemeyer Verlag, 1963), p. 22 (emphasis in the text). The English translation, *Being and Time,* by John Macquarrie and Edward Robinson (New York: Harper & Row, 1962) gives the pagination of the German original as well.

6. This is a point that Hans Jonas treats in his interpretation of a Pauline passage ("The good that I would. . . . ") under the

question of who the "I" there is. Hans Jonas, "The Abyss of the Will," *Philosophical Essays* (Englewood Cliffs, N.J.: Prentice-Hall, 1974), pp. 335–48; published also in James M. Robinson, ed., *The Future of Our Religious Past* (New York: Harper & Row, 1971).

7. The "transcendental schema" is the "third thing," which is both intellectual and sensible, homogeneous, on the one hand, with the category and, on the other, with the appearance. *Critique of Pure Reason,* B177/A138.

8. See L. M. Vail, *Language and Ontological Difference* (University Park, Pa.: Pennsylvania State University Press, 1972), p. 158.

9. *KD*, I/1, pp. viii, ix (Foreword).

10. Eberhard Jüngel, *Gott als Geheimnis der Welt* (Tübingen: J.C.B. Mohr [Paul Siebeck], 1977), p. 385.

11. *Identity and Difference,* trans. Joan Stambaugh (New York: Harper & Row, 1969, two-language edition), pp. 113, 114.

12. The term first appears in *Vom Wesen des Grundes,* but the difference is already mentioned in *Sein und Zeit,* p. 4. See Vail, pp. 5, 105.

5

MAX A. MYERS

Toward What Is
Religious Thinking Underway?

I

In what might seem a reversal of the deconstructionist
program, I want to ask not about the past history of
religious thought,* but about its future, not about its
whence but about its whither. Such a question will be
helpful, I think, because many people seem to have the
impression that while deconstruction may be a useful
procedure for engaging in a kind of archeology of thought it
can do very little to advance thought along its path. What
better way, one might ask, to overcome such a
presupposition than to ask the question concerning the end,
the goal of thought, that state of affairs which would, when
attained, satisfy thought? An additional, and to my mind
equally important, reason for asking this question is that it
is seldom asked in contemporary religious thought. The
question that is asked, and asked with great frequency, is
the question of the beginning, the starting point of thought.

---

* I deliberately use the term "religious thinking" throughout this essay
rather than the term "theology." For reasons which will, I hope, become
clear below, I wish to signal a change from the object studied in the
philosophical and theological tradition of the West and the method used
to study it. I would not claim that "theology" could not be reinterpreted,
indeed, one of the consequences of the last part of this paper is that it
could be. "Religious thinking" is more congruent with the language of
the text, at any rate. Similar considerations apply for the use of the term
"philosophy of religion."

Especially is this question asked in the form of a search for a method. Indeed, since the dawn of the modern age in the West with the work of Descartes and Bacon, thought has come more and more under the influence of this search for a method and its concomitant presuppositions. About this overriding concern for methodology we will have more to say shortly; here I wish to advise the reader of some of the, perhaps, unique perspectives which add special features to the course of my own thought about and with deconstructionists. For years, I resisted the style of thought lately known as deconstructionist in the name of my own blend of Hegel, Marx, and Christianity. However, the force of events in the last half of the decade just ended and my dissatisfaction with my own previous position, together with a reading of Nietzsche, Derrida, and especially Heidegger, led me to perceive the necessity for some fundamental readjustments and modifications in that position. Conversion, with its implications of a repudiation of the past and a sharp turn to the new, would be far too radical a term for this process. What follows should make it clear that I still find much of value in Marxist thought and much to disagree with in, for example, Derrida. Instead, I have come to see the pertinency of asking certain questions which earlier had seemed irrelevant, most particularly the question concerning technology and its uncanny accomplice, nihilism. Rather than give this question up to conservative, or even reactionary thought, I think that it must be taken up and addressed by any thought that hopes to speak to the contemporary world. Further, since the question of nihilism arises as an event in Western history it leads, perforce, to a concern with the logic of the process which led to its appearance and which might lead to its sublation. What makes this question particularly poignant for religious thought is the close connection between this process and theology, just as what gives it a special relevance for Marxist thought is its connection with the rise of capitalism. In both cases, an attunement to the basic problematic of the age means a reconstruction of thought as well as its deconstruction. Hence, the deconstructionists concern for the unfolding of thought in the beginning leads to a reconstructionist concern for the end of thought and an agonistic relationship with two modes of thought within the expanse of the Western tradition, the Christian and the Marxist.

II

The modern world has been dominated by a search for the valid beginnings of thought in various realms: religion, philosophy, natural science, politics, economics, art, law, etc.[1] Typically, this search has expressed itself not only as a search for a new standpoint but also as a search for a new way, a new method. The intuitive pattern of thought here is clear enough. In order to make a new beginning one must have some means of orienting oneself. If one does not, how can one tell if the new beginning is right? Further, since a beginning is only a beginning if something else follows, one must have some means of checking and justifying the steps taken from this new beginning. How can one discover whether the relations between the steps are valid or not, whether, indeed, the steps are going in the right direction? This question, along with the consideration that the subsequent steps themselves serve, in some sense, to justify the beginning, led to the gradual displacement of the question of the beginning by the question of the correct method. The question of the correct method, in turn, came to be replaced or constituted by the question of a correct criterion. In philosophy, for example, the two main trends of the early modern age, rationalism and empiricism, shared a formally similar methodology; both separated complex wholes into elemental units upon the validity of which the relevant complex whole rested. They differed, of course, with respect to the estimation of the nature of this valid elemental unit; for rationalism, it was a clear and distinct idea or else a self-evident truth; for empiricism, it was a sense-datum.[2] Over time, these positions changed internally and externally, but the way of thinking was fixed as one of separation and justification.

If this movement is reflected upon, an interesting point appears. The question of a new beginning, as we have noted, has two aspects: that of taking up a standpoint and that of the justificatory method. The standpoint depends upon the method as the means for its establishment and fulfillment. Equally significant, however, is the fact that the method itself depends upon the adoption of the standpoint, that is, the acceptance, nominally tentative, of an attitude toward reality which would allow the employment of the method.[3] This is, of course, a variant of the double-reflective movement usually labeled the "hermeneutical circle." Rather than merely labeling it, however, which would do little to further our investigation here, it would be more fruitful to probe into its unique meaning for the modern age and its relation to the history of human thought.

If we inquire about the meaning of the quest for method in the modern age and its unique importance here, one factor must receive special consideration: the emergence of mathematico-scientific thought to a dominant position in culture.[4] This factor has long been remarked, of course, although its meaning has been for centuries a matter of controversy. In the first place, it is clear that the relationship between what we have called standpoint and method is a reflective if not a fully dialectical one. Specifically, humans have adopted the mathematico-scientific perspective on the world and that has led them to a discovery and articulation of a corresponding method and that method in turn has further defined their standpoint and so on. The emergence of the search for a method of thought in all realms has arisen from the self-consciousness of the mathematico-scientifically situated subject and an attempt at a fulfilled self-understanding by that subject.[5] One of the most profound efforts for this fulfilled self-understanding appeared at the very inauguration of the modern age in the thought of Thomas Hobbes. Hobbes, explicitly and self-consciously, proffered an "atomic" analysis of society and individual human being which was to a degree seldom realized.[6] In fact, Hobbes's program, in its radicalism and coherency may serve us, as it did his contemporaries, as exemplary of the tendency of the modern spirit to attain self-consciousness in its purest form.

Hobbes's attempt at a consistent extension of the self-understanding of the mathematico-scientific standpoint was resisted, however, as were subsequent, less radical attempts down to and including nineteenth-century positivism,[7] in the name of the autonomy of the cultural sphere. The bearers of this resistance were art, metaphysics, and religion, and, to a somewhat lesser degree, history and the nascent social sciences. The common defense of these fields was that the scientific standpoint and its methodology were not competent or capable of doing justice to the standpoints required by these realms.[8] This defense, however, proved to be ambiguous and in the end fatal. To use a military metaphor, it was tactically brilliant but strategically disastrous. The very use of the notion of a privileged standpoint for aesthetic experience, religious experience, etc., gave the broader field over to the enemy by tacitly accepting its assumptions. To assert that there is a unique religious standpoint, for example, leads one into the quest for a method formally similar to the scientific quest for a method, since that is the only type of method that will gain currency in the public realm of discourse. This moment can be pinpointed in much modern philosophy of religion which has been in a kind of junior partnership with the philosophy of science.[9] Further, the very substantiality, let alone the necessity, of such a religious standpoint becomes questionable. If the consequences of adopting a religious standpoint conflict with those of the mathematico-scientific standpoint, the tendency is to assume that the religious standpoint is illusory or that it can be subordinated to some other explanation. A similar fate befalls the exponent of aesthetic experience, historical knowledge, etc. In all these cases, what at first appeared as irreducible and objective becomes subordinate and subjective and then becomes emptied of meaning.

If this much can be said for the unique configuration of the modern world, what can we say for the historical career of thought? Elsewhere, I have argued that thought can be viewed as significant action which, adopting the terms of Jürgen Habermas, may be divided into two types, instrumental and dialogical.[10] Briefly, the distinction is as follows: instrumental action is unilateral action which shapes reality for the sake of some predetermined goal; dialogical action is reciprocal action between at least two individuals whose primary aim is understanding, in the course of which or as a result of which some other aim may emerge. Essentially, I would argue, dialogical thought is prior to instrumental thought in the sense that instrumental thought is derivative of dialogical thought and acts on its behalf. It is through the event of understanding that meaning appears in the world, and it is meaning for which instrumental activity is engaged. However, once the event character of meaning and understanding is obliterated or forgotten as it is when meaning is identified with certain basic symbols and the manipulation of the symbols is misunderstood as understanding, the relationship between dialogical and instrumental activity is inverted.

Such an inversion, it is clear, took place at the beginning of the modern age with the rise of the mathematico-scientific standpoint and its corresponding method. However, this reversal did not happen all at once and without preparation. Rather, the basis for this reversal had been laid much earlier with the foundation of Western thought in Greek metaphysics.[11] Without such a preparation of the soil, so to speak, such a process would never have occurred. Behind the modern "standpoint" stood the notion of a worldless subject capable of controlling its relation to a world and to the realm of the Ideas, and behind the notion of method as use of criterion stood the notion of the manipulation of these Ideas and of the world in order to bring about some state of affairs, usually a relationship of correspondence between the view of the Ideas entertained and the world. Further, and not less importantly, the attitude adopted by the subject is one which takes up a view of the Ideas and of the world, which is capable of re-presenting them, when it chooses and for its purposes. It is this relationship of re-presentation, along with its correlative sort of presence, which creates the possibility of establishing a distance between the subject and its world. This distance, for its part, spatializes the relationship between subject, world, and Ideas and objectivates them. In this way, space and the beings present and re-presented as present in space becomes the controlling relation. Time, for its part, passes from being the way things happen and meaning appears into a relationship defined by the measurement, the criterion of spatial beings, e.g., the sun and its movements. Time is interpreted no longer as spread out over past, present, and future but as congealed into one point-instant, the same point-instant which is the basis for the mathematico-scientific standpoint, the ideal limit and the ultimate individuating element. This point-instant, as the "now" or the "here and now," also provides the most certain foundation for all knowledge, since what is beyond all possibility of doubt and corrigibility is what is present to our intuition at that point, what is immediate to our look now. Once this experience finds language, the magic circle is broken and mediation enters in and with mediation the possibility of corruption and error. Language, which by its nature is public, always betrays the essentially private certainty of the moment of intuition. At best language cannot make present, only the look can do that, but can only re-present what has been seen from a particular standpoint. Reality is, at bottom, what can be seen, is *eidos* ("form"), and its ideality comes from its being capable of being seen again. In modern philosophy, this *eidos* becomes the object standing over against a subject which is adequately equipped to know it and is also most real in the present. For this subject the past is a now that has been present and can only be represented in language, just as the future is only a now that is not yet but that can also be re-presented. Retention and protention are not aspects of the moment of the self inhabiting a world with other selves but are only a present activity of the isolated subject.

This interpretation of reality and of the self's relation to it which seems so obvious and familiar to the modern world is, in fact, a construction built up in the tradition of Western metaphysics; that is, it is a historical construction. It represents the development of a particular way of interpreting temporality, not as presence but as the present. It expresses a decision to treat memory and expectation not as traces of the past and of the future but as signs indicating and referring to a present that is no more or that is not yet. It is a choice to treat as derivative or unimportant all the modes, including time, in which what is other than the private experience of the present are actually effective in our lives. To sum up, it is an attempt to exclude alterity from the most real and most certain moments of life, including, perhaps especially including, the moment of death. Nietzsche has exposed the secret of Western metaphysics, the reason why it has constructed such a supersensible realm of Ideas and God independent of time and devalued the earthly sensible world. He named it "revenge against time and its 'It was'."[12] Vengeance is the essentially reactive persecution of that which harms us, which causes us to suffer. Time in its passing is the primary example of such suffering since in time's perishing we come to the limits of our instrumental activity, of our ability to dominate. What has happened is gone and we cannot bring it back, do what we will. To what extent this experience depends upon and to what extent it is constitutive of the Western metaphysical conception of time as a series of "now-points" is a question that need not concern us now. What occupies our attention here is the inability to affirm the event character of reality, because it so obviously and painfully eludes our instrumental activity. Only dialogical activity with its delays, its anticipations and waiting, its risks and surprising fulfillments is capable of being attuned to time. Instrumental activity is a response which refuses to wait, which declines the risks of dialogue and its time, which cannot forgive the pain and humiliation of loss and consequently erects an eternal self-presence in the stead of time. It is full of spite and hatred for that which passes away and therefore devalues anything which bears the mark of becoming. There is, it must be admitted, something heroic and beautiful in this refusal, yet it is essentially an inauthentic and petty response. It is inauthentic because in this response the human being does not become what human beings are, and petty because by this response the human closes off possibilities rather than opens to them. For these reasons, Nietzsche says through the character of Zarathustra that deliverance from revenge against time is the bridge by which to pass over to the Overman, the one who does not say no to earthly life and time, but says yes, and with that yes puts a closure to Western metaphysics.

Dialogical activity, if taken seriously, leads to the deconstruction of the set of metaphysical assumptions which had been given birth by the dominance of instrumental activity. Once dialogical activity is seen as primary then the pattern shifts, the look is no longer primary and time is no longer a point-instant. What becomes primary is an open and reciprocal relationship between self and self, self and other selves, and self and world, in which time is the way that this relationship happens, its spreading horizon. The epistemological subject, self-present to itself and to a present object at a "now-point" is seen to be derivative and not the fundamental ground of all certainty. This process of the deconstruction, the historical dismantling and overcoming of the world view of the Western metaphysical tradition was begun by Hegel, especially in the *Phenomenology of Spirit,* and continued by Heidegger and Derrida. Recently, Richard Rorty, working out of the Anglo-American linguistic tradition has added precision and relevance for English-speaking thinkers to this process in his *Philosophy and the Mirror of Nature.*[13] Using Wittgenstein and Dewey as well as Heidegger, Rorty has examined the use of the epistemological subject and its correlated problematic and has shown that they rest on several interpretations which are or should be open to radical questioning.[14] In his reinterpretation of what philosophy should be, Rorty proposes that it be conceived no longer as wisdom, the search for first principles, but as conversation. Without making the same point about instrumental action as the basis for the epistemological construction, Rorty does reject the latter and comes to advocate essentially the same type of dialogical action as we have. On one point, however, I think that Rorty must be questioned. After stating, correctly, that philosophy is conversation from which principles are derived and not vice versa, Rorty goes on to claim that this means that there can be no criteria for conversation.[15] Now if we grant the first part of this statement, there is obviously a sense in which that is true, namely, that we cannot simply judge each conversation with a ready-made criterion which has arisen apart from conversation. However, in order for the conversation to be a real conversation and not simply a game of strategy or an act of coercion, there are certain conditions that must be met: all discussants must be competent in all relevant respects to enter in the dialogue; there must be knowledge of and adherence to the norms for discourse; there must be reciprocal respect and openness, etc. Now these are not, I assume, what Rorty had in mind when he called for criterionless thinking, since his use of criterion is derived from the epistemological tradition. Still, it would seem to be artificial to insist that these are not criteria of a genuine dialogue but something else (what?) and it would be simply wrong to say that these, or some list like them, were irrelevant to judging when a real dialogue was taking place and not propaganda or some other distorted discourse. It is precisely at this point, I think, that both Marxism and psychotherapy have an essential contribution to make, by showing both how distorted conversation occurs, through ideology and repression, and how interventions can be made to correct it. But this criticism, though real, is minor compared with the tremendous advance made by Rorty's book in showing how three major contemporary movements in philosophy, represented by Wittgenstein, Heidegger, and Dewey, cohere in rejecting the assumptions of traditional Western metaphysics.

Such a view as that outlined above provides the horizon on which the human could turn away from the event of meaning/being, or, perhaps better, the event of meaning/being could turn itself away, and instrumental activity become the dominant relation. Once such a turn had been taken, the adoption of the mathematico-scientific standpoint by the early modern thinkers appears less than revolutionary, indeed, if we may put it so, as an unfolding of the destiny of thought in the West. From such a posture, then, how could the goal of thinking appear? Theoretically, it would be to enframe the world as the place which can be represented and brought into correct correlation with the particular view of Ideas assumed. Practically, it would be to shape the world "artistically" so that this view of Ideas may be realized. The linchpin, however, of both theory and practice is the control of both Ideas and world by the subject, which control Nietzsche named power. The issue devolves, according to Nietzsche, on the will to power, not the Ideas which are simply the stuff on which power is exerted, but the will to power. Nor is this simply a subjective will, since the subject is itself a social fiction, but a pure will to power, a force whose bearer awaits us in the future. This is the real meaning of Nietzsche's proclamation of the death of God, the dialectical overcoming of the metaphysical Idea-God, a supersensible being like any other being, by the appearance of its truth, the hidden will to power.[16]

In terms of our discourse here, the will to power is enacted in instrumental action and has extended the sphere of its dominance throughout history. Its broader meaning was realized when humans, having displaced dialogical action in their own affairs, reinterpreted traditional religious symbols in their own image. God was no longer the covenant partner, dialogue with whom assembled earth and sky and mortals, but became a subject manipulating the world, who could in turn be manipulated—a fetish. This turn was decisive for the history of the West, and perhaps not only of the West. The real God became alienated from humans and became the unknown God. In this real God's place were set up idols which were held to represent his presence, rules of practical and cultic activity which were held to mirror and participate in his laws for the universe and, in place of humans responding to meaning from their partner, subjects of an apotheosized Subject exercising his power on them for a unilaterally chosen goal.[17] In place of the legends of Genesis in which God and Adam and Eve dialogue with one another, responding to one another's saying, in alienated religion humans worship projections of their own instrumental activity, making the earth and their partners over into an instrumental ensemble. Two peculiarities of the Genesis story may illustrate this dialogical relationship. In Genesis, it is not God but Adam who bestows names on the creatures, while in Plato and the *Tao Te Ching,* for example, there is still a notion of the alternate view, that the names of things are imposed by an alien power. In Genesis, also, the image of God is not reason or will as later theological thought held but sexuality, communication between opposites.[18]

Marx and Feuerbach, then, were correct when they developed a critical theory of religion as humanity's alienation from its own "species-being" (*Gattungswesen*).[19] They were wrong, however, when they followed the path of their positivist contemporaries in identifying the typical essence of man with instrumental activity. In Marx's view, which proved more significant than Feuerbach's in the end, the goal of religious thinking was to dissolve the alienated and alienating God, belief in whom put only illusory flowers on the chains of those social conditions which prevented the manipulation and enjoyment of the world by all instrumental subjects. In Marx's image of the future communist society in the third volume of *Capital,* the metabolism between man and nature was one controlled by all humans, in which each person would find happiness in the satisfaction of the needs of all. Does not this image of Marx introduce an element at once positivistic and idealistic, in the derogatory sense, which contributes to human alienation? Was not Nietzsche nearer the mark when he identified the true source of human alienation as the will to power, which Marx's discourse only served to obscure? In spite of Marx's inestimable service in disillusioning humans about the real nature of their cultures and societies and in spite of his historical method, one must assert that his instrumental subject, which *was* the truth of capitalist society, hid from humanity its real dialogical essence.[20]

Nietzsche, however, in revealing the real subject as the will to power, missed as well the dialogical. The goal of religious thinking in his view, was to await the new subject able to embrace the will to power as the monstrous, the prodigious, the unnamable apocalyptic, to which he gave the name Overman, "Caesar with the soul of Christ."[21] There can be little doubt that Nietzsche was giving voice to an, perhaps the, determinative reality of the life of the West which had largely remained unsaid and unconscious. However, Nietzsche's style, the very style which made him such an astute interpreter, was not attuned to the genuine dialogical and remained, like Marx's, an eschatology without a valid apocalyptic.

The unfolding of Western thought has arrived, after the substitution of instrumental thought for dialogical thought, at a point of impasse. The history of this thought as metaphysics has reached its dialectical unraveling with the end of metaphysics as the logical outcome of its beginning in Plato. Thinking has become a representation of beings in the world according to conventional grammars which can, of course, now be conducted by machines. The question of standpoint and method of modern thought has become an infinite play of reflection. Only those adopting a standpoint can use the method and only those using the method can adopt the standpoint. One might object that there is, however, the small matter of existential reference which this view neglects to take into account. But those who would so object do not see that the "existential reference" as an indication of the relation between a word or proposition and a state of affairs is itself part of the method. Truth itself for modern thought, and here it follows a line of development that reaches back to Greek metaphysics, becomes entirely a matter of such a correspondence between an object, a "thing," and the mind or the intention, as formulated in a word, a *verbum,* whether internal or external. Truth as presence consigns to oblivion the older understanding of truth as revelation or "un-hiddenness" (*alētheia*). In such a landscape the question of meaning does not appear at all, save in the accepted form of a relation of representation. This is the "end of metaphysics."[22]

Religious thinking, for its part, has little essential to add to the drama. Religious thinking, as theology, has from its beginning and with few exceptions followed the lead of metaphysics. The word *God* was taken to refer to a being, like other beings in sharing the same predicates indicative of reality although to an eminently higher degree. God is easily, all too easily, identified with the being of all beings which these beings are taken to represent, whether as intellect knowing itself or as will is less important here than that this being is self-present in an eternal now, just as is each self-conscious creature. Western theology thus synthesized the God of religious tradition and the being of the metaphysical tradition with little trouble, covering up inconsistencies, as for example that between timelessness and divine love, by a long litany of metaphysical compliments. Yet, God's function was to assure that the laws of the universe or the grammar of our words remained constant. The doctrine of analogy, one of the most creative efforts to render this situation comprehensible, came to wreck on the impossible project of making our representational words refer to the unspeakable. The confluence of these two traditions, the metaphysical and the theological, led to the formation of the one tradition Heidegger called the "onto-theo-logical."[23]

The doctrine of analogy is one of the most sophisticated ways of attempting to escape the consequences of the traditional onto-theo-logical position. The strength and appeal of the doctrine of analogy is that it clearly and explicitly recognizes the major failure of the metaphysical view; namely, that God or being is not a being like any other being. Hence, the concepts and categories drawn from ordinary experience are not applicable, in the same sense, to God or being, and must be used analogically. As a result, it is held that there is a relation of proportionality between the different realms of being which makes our discourse intelligible. There is an obvious similarity between the analogical view and the position developed here, insofar as analogy is understood along the lines of a metaphor. Yet, that is not the fundamental point of the doctrine of analogy, and it would be a misunderstanding to conceive it so. For the doctrine of analogy understands the logos, not as the gathering of meaning in a dialogical event, as we have attempted to explicate it, but as a *locus,* a plenitude of meaning from which all our meanings are derivative. This is simply, though, a recasting of what we have called the traditional tripartite view of reality, wherein meaning resides in a transcendent realm and this world merely echoes it, more or less faintly. Harold Bloom has been one of the most forthright critics of the doctrine of analogy, particularly in the field of literary criticism where he has pointed out its influence on the interpretation of texts.[24] We cannot go into his literary ideas here in any detail, but we should take note of his alternative proposal, what he calls an agonistic reading rather than an analogical reading. Briefly, rather than seeing the meaning emerge as the original text comes more clearly into view, Bloom suggests that truth and meaning emerge as the reader struggles with the text, that is, questions it, develops counterpositions and makes further connections. This stops somewhat short of the view taken here, but it could certainly be developed into such a view. We may take it though as an indication of the paucity of the doctrine of analogy and the need to resist its somewhat seductive blandishments, the need, in other words, to make a break with it and to develop an alternative agonistic hermeneutic.

In such a situation, toward what can we say that religious thinking is underway? If we mean by "religious thinking," the mode of thinking practiced by traditional theology or philosophy of religion, the answer is nothing. Nothing might seem to be no answer, but it is not. Nothing would be no answer if we remained within the tradition of the West where nihilism is without value, an impossibility to be shunned at all costs. If nihilism means the senseless repetition of words and action which leads to more of the same, then it would be no answer, even it if were an accurate depiction of our era. But even in senseless repetition, as in a totally technological universe where instrumental activity is all, nothing has the possibility of fecundity. Buber, and after him Heidegger, have pointed to the experience of the uncanny precisely in such a technological world.[25] To experience the nothingness of a self-referring system opens up a difference between the things and that which is no-thing. When thinking then, stunned though it be through its habits of thinking things referring to other things, turns to the no-thing, it begins to respond to a call unlike other calls. Thinking then knows that it cannot respond to the no-thing with its usual controlling responses. At that point, it must make the movements that allow meaning into its world. These movements, however, presuppose that a clearing has been made, that the obstacles placed in the path of communication have been removed.[26]

The first step forward for religious thinking is, accordingly, a step back which can release the present from the burden of the past. Heidegger has called this step back the "destruction of metaphysics" and has viewed it as a necessary prolegomenon for thinking.[27] This demand has also, of course, been repeated by the hermeneutical school, for example, Gadamer, and by the deconstructionist movement, especially Derrida.[28] One might point out in passing what is hardly a secret, namely, that Hegel had already initiated such a procedure in his dialectical thought. The first movement of dialectical thought is to challenge the infirm glory of the positive moment in order to open thought for a more valid moment.[29] To say this much hardly provides an answer to our question, though, since religious thinking is not on its way to mere destruction but to meaning, to the appearance of being.

III

We seem to have returned to the question of the goal of religious thinking with which we began. But this return, like all returns, is marked by a difference, even as it asks the same question. For now, we have recognized the nullity of the modern elevation of instrumental action over dialogical action. The truth of this moment has turned out to be the will to power but a will to power which, ironically, destroys the very subject whose project it was. The will to power and the subject are enmeshed in the very dissolving reflecting-reflection of the standpoint and methodology. This is a characteristic conundrum of modern thought, a correlation of polar opposites, neither of which can exist without the other, but both of which, if pursued ruthlessly, destroy the other. This conundrum Georg Lukács called (not wholly inaccurately) the antinomy of bourgeois society and its thought.[30] I say not wholly inaccurately because, while the outcome is most evident in bourgeois society, it is not con-fined to that society but appears in other modes in other stages of society as well. The determining contradiction, I would hold, is the resolve on the part of the subject to achieve its own foundation, or in more religious language, a striving for self-justification. Linguistically, this antinomy appears in the paradox of meaning. The subject intends something and utters words to carry this meaning, yet the meaning of the utterance is always something other than the meaning originally intended. To be sure, this frustration appears in a peculiarly violent and systematic form in a capitalist society where meaning itself becomes a commodity, that is, a product produced primarily for its exchange value not its use value. In such a society, as Marx pointed out, the intention of the primary producers is alienated in the final product and all meaning is resident in capital, a self-referential system of accumulation where all questions of meaning are subordinated to the "golden rule" of the capitalist, accumulation of exchange value for its own sake. On this question, as we have noted above, Marxism while correct in its critical diagnosis has proved little better in its proposed reconstruction. Ignoring for the moment the thorny question of the actual justice of Marxist regimes in practice, historical Marxism simply assumes that by recognizing the instrumental role of the producers the alienation of meaning will disappear. This has not been borne out in practice as the history of socialist regimes since the Second World War has shown. To be fair, we must note that there are theoretical options in some forms of Marxism which elevate the dialogical principle to primacy, yet these options have largely remained unexplored and, in any case, have been disowned both by official Marxist thought and, in the case of Lukács and others, by their originators. Thus, in socialist thought, as in capitalist, meaning is produced in the form of socially useful objects, tools, art, or propaganda, whose value is set by a self-referential system under the guise of humanity.

Marx's thought, however, like any healthy thought remains multivalent, full of digressions and self-criticisms which mock any scholastic encapsulation of it, even if that is done in the name of scientific historical materialism. One such feature, relevant to our point here, is his notion that, in a communist society the form of society, the shape of its economic and social relations, would emerge spontaneously from the content. In Marx's view, every other form of society has been marked by a contradiction between the form and the content, the form being imposed on the content instead of developing from it.[31] This has had the consequence of stifling the development of the content, especially classes. The meaning of liberation would be the overcoming of the repressive form of society, and the dominant class which maintained it, and its reconstitution from below, through the cooperative action of the actual producers, the working class. Although Marx never developed this insight in any thorough way, beyond the dialectic of the proletariat as the bearer of the universal interests of society, it has remained as a kind of criticism of any merely instrumental view of society and, in fact, is similar to the task of deconstruction. For deconstruction, too, even though it would be critical of the form-content dichotomy, understands the shape of society to deform its reality and attempts to release the forces from below, through a return to dialogical activity.

The ultimate result of the Enlightenment, or Renaissance, identification of knowledge with power was quite the reverse of its surface appearance. Ostensibly, the purpose of science was to further the range of the action of the subject and thereby to strengthen the subject. However, the scientific ideal for gaining this knowledge was for the human to become a mirror of nature, to reflect reality "objectively" without the interposition of any prejudices but also without any passionate affirmation or negation involving the whole self. In fact, for the true scientist there is no place for the self, only "points of view" which are simply constituted by a confluence of forces at a particular "now." Even those who are nominally in charge of giving the scientific project direction are themselves in the grip of powerful forces, the drive to accumulate, the drive to extend and make more efficient the instrumental grid, the drive for pleasure and comfort. There are, to be sure, conflicts engendered by these forces, and these may give the appearance of agonizing and dramatic decisions. Particularly is this the case with respect to those occasions when the forward thrust of the technological ensemble threatens the ideological trace of some previous event of meaning: medical ethics abounds with examples of this sort but they are to be found in all realms into which technology intrudes, that is to say, in all of human life. I do not mean to suggest that such occasions are not experienced as real dilemmas with pain and renunciation for those involved, but normally they involve merely a grappling with isolated problems rather than addressing the totality of the modern epoch. It is this that often gives them the appearance of a rear-guard, obscurantist character and predooms them to defeat. Like their opponents who argue in favor of technology, the opponents of technology identify the essence of technology with instruments, tools, and machines and do not look for the essence of technology in the historical prevalence of the mathematico-scientific as the way in which being presents itself in our epoch. Apart from the inconsistencies and superficialities into which this throws the opponents of technology, this has the ironic result that they are often left arguing for positions whose historical unraveling led to precisely the dominance of technology which they are combating.

The way out of this quandry is not to continue with the sterile round of action and reaction within the construction of Western metaphysics but to step back, to disassemble the modern construction and to clear a path for dialogical action. Only such a radical step back can stop the wheel from spinning idly and meaninglessly, and only in a rebirth of dialogical action can the self become responsive and alive once again. The cure for the specifically modern paralysis of the will is not the heroic attempt to create values in isolation but a real conversation with the self, the world and other selves in which each self can find its responsive and responsible center. Moreover, and just as importantly, this reclamation of the responsive self is also a reawakening of the sensual self. For once the center is shifted from a supersensible realm of Ideas or God to dialogical activity, the look ceases to be the center of attention and loses its hypnotic quality. As energy is rechanneled from the phallic-

intrusive look to other areas of experience, other, sup-
pressed, modes of bodily life become charged with interest
and the whole self is called into play. The genital, monumental, immortal fixation with its denial of time, death, and
becoming is subverted by the sensual, the playful with its
acceptance and affirmation of life and death. Dialogue calls
forth this response. It is impossible to be in dialogue with
the world without becoming involved with the physical
rhythms of sun, wind, and water, smells, sights and
sounds. Similarly, it is impossible to come into conversation
with other selves without the embodiment of waiting,
anticipation, distance and proximity, letting go and bearing up.

A major task of religious thinking, therefore, is to
criticize the unstable center of modern thought, its turn to
instrumental action as the sole valid type of action with its
correlative aspect of self-reference or self-justification. In
order to do this, as we have indicated, religious thinking
must sublate the criterion principle of the former type of
thinking. This is especially difficult inasmuch as modern
thought demands a criterion and its associated elements as
the price of admission to contemporary discussion. Once
this demand is acceded to, though, the game is up for
religious thinking since it has entered the very language
system that it has to overcome. If the demand is refused,
however, then religious thinking is relegated to the sector
of the irrational or the occult. For this reason, religious
thinking must begin with a dialectical destruction of
modern thought, as we have attempted to do, through a
reconstruction of its moments. In this way, one can step
back into the original relation to being and meaning.

Is this last step possible? Certainly, the opinion of some
deconstructionists, such as Derrida, is that it is not.[32]
Moreover, the very search for such an original, unmediated
relationship to being is held up as an essential characteristic
of the nostalgic "age of the sign." If it were simply nostalgic,
a desire for a primal regression, such an opinion would be
justified. As Hegel pointed out in his *Logic,* the unmediated

appearance of being is indistinguishable from nothing, as absolute plenitude would be identical with absolute emptiness, there being nothing by definition to distinguish them.[33] But the relation with absolute being is abstract, a beginning of thought, not the end of a search. To take it as such an end would itself be an alienation, since between such an abstract monstrosity and humanity as little meaning could be discerned as between humanity and the eschatological Overman. Does this mean then that one is driven back to the realm of becoming, a self-referential play of appearances, a discordant raging of opposing forces, as Derrida appears to suggest?[34] It would mean this if such a relation were the only sense available of an originary relation to being. I would like to suggest that religious thinking is on the way to another sort of relationship to originating being and meaning.

I would like to suggest that originating being and meaning appear in a dialogical relationship between humanity and the world and between humans. The *locus* of this relationship is not a place at all, or not a place simply, since that would inevitably bind it to a spatial unit, but an event, a "coming-to." It is an event which assembles earth and mortals, human and human; it brings them together and makes them whole. It is not self-referential precisely because it does not refer at all, but presences. It is not self-justifying because it comes when it comes without and in spite of attempts by the self to control it. Its bearer is the disclosing, opening word, a word whose essence is this unveiling and which may or may not find utterance in a vibrating vocal chord. This word may find utterance in a vibrating leaf or in ripples on a pond, as well as in human gesture. What we call language is the attempt to respond to this primal saying. What we call understanding is our participation in this meaning. Our insight is our share in the flashing-in of this shining.[35] This event does not happen in abstraction from the world or other humans, but in a linguistic, understanding, insightful relationship with them, when we are open and our partner is open, in other words, in dialogue.

Speaking is always speaking about something. Hence, utterances are always capable of propositional analysis. But this analysis is always an abstraction from the speech act itself and as such the meaning of the act eludes it. The attempt, common today, to reduce the meaning of an utterance to a proposition which can be held to represent a state of affairs, to be a sign, is understandable if one adopts an instrumental view. In such an analysis, the meaning becomes manipulable, subject to the control of a subject. But does not such a conception of meaning lead to meaninglessness, as we have argued above? Nor is the situation much changed if we adopt instead the view that an utterance expresses the inner state, intention, or emotion of a subject. This too, without doubt, is a possible abstraction from an utterance. There is no utterance which does not express the subject. But, we must ask, does not such a conception also presuppose an instrumental view, no less than the propositional? Finally, we might suggest, following John Austin's notion of the illocutionary or performative, that the utterance brings about an interpersonal relationship.[36] When, for example, we promise we are not, or not only, informing someone or expressing ourselves but are creating expectations and claims in and on persons. Obviously, one can view speaking correctly as doing this also. It should be obvious, as well, that such a conception is closer to our notion of the dialogical than the other two candidates, and that it is a notion which shows great promise, particularly as a corrective to the current infatuation with the propositional. However, it should be noted that such a speech act depends for its meaning on conformity to preestablished linguistic forms or conventions. Are we prepared to say that speaking is mere conformity to convention? To put the question in a sharper form, would not such conformity be compatible with meaninglessness? Moreover, to the extent that one recognizes, as one must, the validity of the propositional and expressive aspects of speaking, the illocutionary aspect cannot claim to be the meaning of speaking. One must make the attempt to find a notion of speaking which integrates these three aspects of utterances, while avoiding the elevation of the epistemological subject and instrumental action to dominance.

Jürgen Habermas has made such an attempt in his recent work on universal pragmatics. After delineating three aspects of the speech act to which the three given above roughly approximate, Habermas goes on to correlate them with different areas of experience.[37] The propositional is correlated with the world or external nature, the expressive is connected with the inner experience of the self, and the interpersonal is related to the world of society and its symbols. Speaking itself is the act of making comprehensible all these realms, to others and to oneself. Understanding, on the other hand, is the act of reconstructing the speech act so as to integrate the world, the self, and society in the same way as the speaker. At this point, Habermas's notion of reconstruction shows its kinship with both Gadamer's hermeneutics and Collingwood's view of historical knowledge as reenactment.[38]

There is actually little to separate Habermas's views from Gadamer's, save the former's greater familiarity with the precisions of Anglo-American linguistic philosophy. Gadamer also holds that understanding is the act of reconstructing the speaker's act through reliving, as it were, the act within the speaker's horizon which implies a translation out of one's own horizon into the speaker's.[39] Habermas is more concerned than Gadamer with the emancipatory direction of speaking and understanding. Understanding implies release from the narrowness of one's own situation into that of another, while speaking enables one to integrate parts of one's experience that were formerly cut off and unnamed. This emancipatory direction shows itself, it seems to me, in Habermas's concern with the communicative competency of each subject, which leads him to be critical of institutional matrices which block the subject's communicating power and leads to an interest in Marxism and psychoanalysis as liberating hermeneutical movements of the oppressed and repressed, respectively.[40]

Despite a general agreement with Habermas on the issues raised by his universal pragmatics, I think that one must ask whether he has gone deeply enough into the acts of speaking-understanding, whether his analysis of meaning is sufficient. One thing seems to me to be clear: understanding is the ability to reconstruct a speech act. Understanding does imply the ability to reenact the speaker's activity as she or he integrates the world, the self and others following the grammar and obeying the institutional rules of a particular social whole. One must be able to see why and how one was led to make the utterances one made, if one is to claim comprehension. In Collingwood's language, one must be able to see the question to which the utterance is an answer.[41] Granted this much, however, one must go on to ask, Is this reconstruction what religious thinking is on the way to? Are we, for example, as religious thinkers aiming at a reconstruction of the speech acts of Jesus in, for example, the parables so that we can rethink them now? The answer, I think, is yes, but that that involves something more that Habermas has not, so far as I know, made manifest. The presupposition that lies beneath our ability to reconstruct Jesus' or Paul's thought is that we are turned to hear the saying that they were turned to hear, just as Jesus and Paul could reconstruct the thought of the prophets or the psalmists by being turned to a partner to whom those earlier speakers were listening. This turning, of course, is not part of the manifest utterance, not even of its deep structure, but is unsaid. It is in this unspoken turning that meaning enters into language. It is this that is the same in their speaking and ours, even as they are different, and it is this sameness that accounts for understanding in spite of difference. In Habermas, the act of understanding is truncated. He seems to presume that it is in our power to integrate the world, the self, and society, while a more adequate account, I would argue, would hold that the meaning comes to us, in an event. What we must still search for, I would hold, is the giving of meaning, the turning of being toward us, in the act of utterance.

If we wish to say that religious thinking is on the way toward a reconstruction of the speech event, we will mean by that the following. First, since it is a reconstruction, we must necessaily deconstruct the utterance. This means that we must take it out of the frame which structures it as it is handed down to us. As long as an utterance is heard in the framework of traditional onto-theo-logy it will remain incapable of giving us meaning. The work of the framing of traditional metaphysics leads to a planetary nihilism, as we have seen above, in which actuality is reduced to a reflected-reflecting will to power. In an ironic manner, history has performed the task of deconstructing the utterance for us. This, however, should not be so surprising since even when being turns away from us, as in a planetary loss of meaning, it is still related to us, since we still are. Thinking which thinks the turning away, especially when it thinks it as nothingness, is beginning to think being in a more primal sense than thinking which thinks of ideas or representations and the grammatical connections between and among them. Thus, to think of the turning away of being is to think of the turning of being to us. We may say, then, that being begins to turn toward us precisely when we begin to think of the turning away of being from us.

At this point, the reconstructive task of thinking has already begun. We are thinking as a response to the same that others have responded to in their thinking and saying. Once we are aware of this, we are in a position to rethink their thoughts and collect their meanings. Only by rethinking and recollecting can our world, which has been shaped by those thoughts and meanings, by their sedimentation in institutions, rules, and language, be assembled. Rethinking our cultural and social past, as the rethinking of our personal past, can enable us to understand the oppressions and repressions of the past and free us from them. However, it is important to stress that we do not understand past actions by placing them in the mechanical framework of a causal nexus. Our rethinking must always be a rethinking in the presence of the source of their original givenness. The fact and the way that being originally gave or held itself in reserve in our past is the note to which we must be attuned. The given act, as we discern it through its witnesses, can then be understood as a response. To the extent that we perceive it as a response, no matter how poor or rich we deem it to be, it becomes meaning-ful and its meaning of course is then released into our lives. Just as, in dialogue with a contemporary, to the extent that I can share in an event of meaning with her or him, which of course involves a reconstruction of that event, to that extent meaning has become an event for me as well. It is not only the past actions of others which are amenable to this kind of reconstruction, but the acts of my contemporaries and myself. In the latter case, as for example in psychotherapy, one is led, usually by or in the presence of another, to reconstruct past actions which have been forgotten because they had a distorted or unacceptable meaning, so that meaning becomes ingredient in them.

It is important to notice that this kind of reconstruction can only take place in a dialogical action; it is not available to instrumental action. One cannot, after the manner of instrumental action, unilaterally manipulate reality in order to attain a previously conceived goal as a technique for reconstructing the event of meaning. In the first place, of course, this is impossible because the meaning is incapable of being clearly conceived beforehand; it manifests itself, when it does manifest itself, only as we listen. Furthermore, the very act of unilaterally manipulating the reality involved means that we are following a private strategy for the attainment of an already selected goal which by its nature closes us off from the opening of meaning. The dialogical nature of this reconstruction means that we must think with, that is be with, the other in an attitude of waiting for and responding to the given. Thus, even when we are rethinking our own past, we are thinking with, being with, an other. As H. Richard Niebuhr pointed out, building on the psychology of George Herbert Mead, the phenomenon of a conscience points us to the dialogical nature of introspection.[42]

Reconstruction, in the sense in which I use it, has the meaning of rebuilding, reassembling what has already been assembled or constructed but which no longer or not yet assembles. The use of the concept of deconstruction is meant, primarily, to indicate first, that this reconstruction is radical, that is, that it does not merely point to an incompleteness but to a fundamental replacing of presuppositions. Second, and perhaps more importantly, it attempts to say that it takes historicity as an epochal movement, where epoch means the way in which meaning/being gives itself or withholds itself. Both the movements of deconstruction and reconstruction are not in the power of any subject although they are both responses of finite beings in which being and meaning manifest themselves. Both moments must go together; neither has meaning apart from the other, yet neither has meaning apart from the saying to which they are a response. In both there is an element of spontaneity and of historicity. The element of historicity appears in the fact that time is the moment of severance from an assemblage, which by that very severance is its past. The element of spontaneity comes in the raising of a question which makes the desevered moment identical with its past.

The word *reconstruction* is deliberately chosen here to include at least an echo of the redemption of thought in concrete existence present in the writings of John Dewey.[43] Although there is much in Dewey's thought that is indefensible, there is a reference to the present and the future proving of a reappropriation of the past that illumines a shade of meaning not adequately brought out by the customary philosophical notions of "thinking." This "pragmatic" aspect is necessary, I think, in order to bring out both the ethical and the dialogical nature of the reconstruction. Our reconstructions must have a practical bearing on existence in order to be authentic. The preconception that thought, like poetry, changes nothing, while a useful admonition to a superficial notion of thought, underestimates the profound service of both thought and poetry. Real reconstruction must enable all speakers to respond to the originary saying. It must treat all speakers with reciprocity and mutuality, as, in short, true participants in dialogue. In this sense, in paying other selves the respect of dialogue, reconstruction implies true democracy. It cannot be satisfied with understanding by a few but must, in its reconstruction, attempt to be understood by all, with the economic, social, and political consequences this would entail. Insofar as ideologies, religious as well as political, block discourse and legitimate instrumental, that is, nondialogical action, they must be criticized by word and deed. Thus, reconstructions must be placed in the public sphere and opened to the discourse of all. Auto-criticism and peer-criticism must be oriented to democratic criticism. Only when the repressed are allowed their voice can the goal of dialogue, understanding, begin to appear. Only when the reified structures of meaning in the society and in the self are deconstructed can the word live. Only the living word can save us.

Already, Paul Tillich had proposed a position similar to that suggested here with his slogan "the God above God," a phrase which was latent in some mystics and in German idealism.[44] Insofar as Tillich meant by that to name the God which was not an ontic being like other beings, a God that is on the other side of the ontological difference, his usage coheres with ours. However, insofar as Tillich connected that formula with his doctrine of the religious symbol and to his theological system of polarity and correlation it remains within the onto-theo-logical tradition of the West in a decisive way. In particular, Tillich's system seems to be radically unhistorical, despite its emphasis on the *kairos,* since in that system everything remains in a dynamic tension between a manifold of polar opposites which apparently never begin or end. It appears to me that Tillich's theology is a more or less clear expression of the antinomic nature of capitalist society, in the same sense in which Lukács argued that Kant's was. Whereas a thoroughly historical interpretation would understand the categories of thought themselves to be a product of creative dialogue, Tillich views these categories as constitutive of thought independently of historical conversation. These features of his thought place Tillich squarely in the metaphysical tradition and compromise our unqualified appropriation of his formula "the God above God." Still, if this saying is related to our earlier discussion of the traces left by an event of meaning it can be reappropriated. For us, God is beyond God in the sense that the names and images of God in our language are real remainders of a visitation whose meaning is not yet played out, where "not yet" refers both to a reserve of meaning and a promise of meaning. It is this reserve and promise, this retention and protention, what we earlier called "the pregnancy of the not," which makes time the horizon of being. This same rhythm can be followed in all dialogical activity where each response is the bearer of a meaning which is reserved and a meaning which is not made manifest until it is released by the other's responses. It is this rhythm which makes the practice of deconstruction both possible and necessary. It is possible because there is always more meaning held in reserve, waiting to be released, than is present in any linguistic construction. At the same time, it is necessary since without such releasement the construction becomes meaning-less, does not come to fruition. With respect to the word *God,* its central place in the construction of the Western onto-theo-logical tradition gives its deconstruction a high significance and also, of course, promises to unlock meaning in a world where absurdity extends its sway daily.

In the process of reconstructing an event of meaning we must recognize the givenness of the past act. Western epistemology has registered this, without being aware of its implications, in its typical name for the contents of the consciousness of the subject, data. But to become fully aware of this means that we think the act and its circumstances as given to us, as a gift. Now, no one would recognize as a gift that which they did not want or need or value, in short that which lacked meaning for them. Contrariwise, when an act is seen as an event with meaning, as an event which assembles the world and self and others, then it does indeed take on the nature of a gift, and its sending becomes a grace-ful event. When giving, after this fashion, which had previously been ignored as a gift becomes a gift, there is forgiveness. We are enabled to accept it as valuable and meaningful, in spite of our previous turning away from it. The lives of others, and our own life become grace-ful, to the extent that we recognize them as given or think them as fore-given. It is a further consequence of this movement that to the extent that we do not accept ourselves and others as fore-given, to that degree we are not capable of discovering meaning in them. Mathematico-scientific thinking, when it rules out any other meaning than the meaning that is willed by the individual, also rules out the experience of the world and the self as given or fore-given. From the point of view such thinking adopts it is right to do so, since outside of the beings treated in its projects, there is nothing. Religious thinking, on the other hand, views this nothing as the turning of being which sends the beings away from us, while still sending the beings. Sartre was right, in one sense, to say of human reality that it is a "useless passion," since humans are not a means to the goal of any other beings' project.[45] The experience of reality as a gift and fore-giveness, however, opens up the possibility of a different kind of action than the instrumental one that Sartre rejects as incompetent to deal with human being, dialogical action.

We must ask, however, whether the implication of this position would lead us to the conclusion that all acts are events of meaning and hence may be reconstructed. Should we not rather hold that some acts are special acts of meaning, special acts of revelation, which illuminate others, themselves being unilluminated? The answer I would give here is that all acts are events of meaning, although no acts are necessarily such. Here, though, we touch on the real answer to the question posed by our title. Religious thinking is on the way toward a thinking which can and does reconstruct all acts, indeed all events, as events of meaning. In such reconstruction, the world, the self, and others are assembled, not through the intentional grasping of these primarily but through being open to what lies in reserve in the unspoken. In this way, each member comes into its own, which is at once coming into its appropriation by the rule of meaning. As long as this event has not occurred, absurdity and oppression will rule. When this event has occurred, meaning and freedom are released. Hence, traditions must be continually questioned, to the end of effecting this release in any and every event.

If religious thinking assumes this way of being, no particular criteria can be erected in order to judge its path, other than the way of dialogue itself. Each person, including, for example, Jesus or Sidharta Gautama, is a partner on this path, one whose learning we can observe and question and, in this questioning, open ourselves for meaning. Of course, those of us in a particular religious tradition may find some fellow learner who is more observable and questionable, that is, more able to bear our questions. Because of the planetary consciousness brought about by the very technology that turns us away from meaning, we may even be approaching a unitive religious consciousness, to adopt a notion of Wilfred Cantwell Smith.[46] I believe this to be the case. I do not, however, think that the meaning of the current unification of humanity's religious consciousness consists in the ability to choose from a rich array of religious traditions the one which pleases us most or coheres best with our presuppositions. Nor do I think that its meaning lies in an eclectic "new religious consciousness" which pieces together from various traditions what seems best in each. Both of these views rest on the same subjectivism which has been the object of criticism here. Both also refuse to adopt the attitude of learning and questioning that is vitally necessary for religious thinking.

Religious thinking is on the way toward meaning only when it is curious enough to question until it can deconstruct the frame of the tradition in which it moves and reconstruct the event of meaning. Today's world makes it possible, perhaps demands, that each individual deconstruct the frame of his or her tradition in dialogue with others deconstructing their traditions. This dialogue is a great aid in this task because others' perspectives on our tradition free us from assumptions otherwise invisible to us. Relativism is avoided insofar as we recognize the same as the meaning of our various acts of reconstruction. At the same time, we are set free to listen for what has been held in reserve in the discourse of our tradition as we hear what others have heard in it.

It is precisely this lack of attention to what has been held in reserve which has led the modern world into ideologies of various sorts. Treating the sayings of the traditions as propositions to be proved and defended, they have been adjusted to the dominant metaphysical habits of the age. The outcome has been a passionate obsession with certainty and self-justification, individually and collectively. But it is of the essence of a dialogue that the selves involved in a dialogue along with their turning-toward one another, turn-toward from a reserving. Each revelation is a revelation of that which is hidden; every appearance is an appearance of an essence, which essences only in appearances. Thus, a reconstruction of an event of meaning must be an opening to that which is held in reserve, the unsaid along with the said. Such an opening to the unsaid is incompatible with certainty and self-justification, since it is as such an opening to that which cannot be projected as a possibility beforehand by the self. Such an opening, for example, I take to be the meaning of the cross for early Christians, especially Paul. For the cross is precisely the event in which Jesus opened and emptied himself and his message, without certainty, to the hiddenness of God behind its appearance. The actuality of the reconstruction of this event in every now is the meaning of the resurrection.

Religious thinking, then, is thinking which is on the way toward an assembling of selves and the world in the act of reconstructing the event of meaning. It is destructive of every idol, every work, or symbol which claims to be the center of a structure of meaning, for the sake of this reconstruction. It is also destructive of every reconstruction which is only a repetition of the earlier event, for it knows that time is the way that being reveals itself and that no one can step into that stream twice. Therefore, it is equally destructive of conventionalism and of that sort of traditionalism which longs for the eternal return of the same. Yet it is traditionalist in a broader sense, since it knows that in its acts of reconstruction the same is present to it. And it is modern in a deeper sense, since it knows that every now is full of its own meaning in a new way. It must take up the task of clearing the path for its fellow selves in order to be open itself, for it is only in dialogue that meaning can appear and thinking become thanking.

NOTES

1. Illustrative texts may be found in René Descartes, *Philosophical Works,* trans. and ed. N. K. Smith (New York: Modern Library, 1958), and Francis Bacon, Essays, *Advancement of Learning and Other Pieces,* ed. R. F. Jones (New York: Odyssey Press, 1937). R. G. Collingwood, *The Idea of History,* ed. B. Knox (Oxford: Oxford University Press, 1956) and Jürgen Habermas, *Theory and Practice,* trans. J. Viertel (Boston: Beacon Press, 1973), have both commented at some length on the rise of modern science and the beginning of modern philosophy in ways comparable to that suggested here.

2. Carle Raschke points to this trend as the "quest for certainty" in Carl Raschke, *The Alchemy of the Word: Language and the End of Theology* (Missoula, Mont.: Scholars Press, 1979), pp. 1–7.

3. Hegel is responsible for this treatment of the analytic method, G. W. F. Hegel, *The Phenomenology of Mind,* trans. J. Baillie (London: Allen and Unwin, 1966).

4. I use the term "mathematico-scientific," following Heidegger, in order to bring out the quantitative-atomic character of modern science as a way of framing the world. Cf. Martin Heidegger, *What Is a Thing?,* trans. W. B. Barton and Vera Deutsch (Chicago: Henry Regnery, 1967) and *The Question Concerning Technology and Other Essays,* trans. W. Lovitt (New York: Harper & Row, 1977).

5. Jürgen Habermas, *Knowledge and Human Interests,* trans. J. J. Shapiro (Boston: Beacon Press, 1971).

6. Illustrative texts may be found in Thomas Hobbes, *Body, Man, and Citizen,* ed. R. S. Peters (New York: Collier Books, 1962).

7. John Stuart Mill, *On the Logic of the Moral Sciences,* ed. H. M. Magid (Indianapolis: Bobbs-Merrill, 1965), represents a classic attempt to ground the "moral" sciences on the scientific method.

8. Hans-Georg Gadamer, *Truth and Method,* trans. G. Barden and J. Cumming (New York: Seabury Press, 1975), and Habermas, *Knowledge and Human Interests,* trace the history of this methodological development, primarily in Germany.

9. Wolfhart Pannenberg, *Theology and the Philosophy of Science,* trans. F. McDonagh (Philadelphia: Westminster Press, 1976), offers a critical account of this process. It is an open question, to my mind at any rate, whether Pannenberg himself does not fall prey to a very sophisticated notion of the position which he criticizes.

10. Max A. Myers, " 'Ideology' and 'Legitimation' as Necessary Concepts for Christian Ethics," *Journal of the American Academy of Religion* 49, no. 2 (June 1981), pp. 187–210.

11. The analysis which follows is substantially derived from Heidegger's thought.

12. From section 2 of *Thus Spoke Zarathustra* in Friedrich Nietzsche, *The Portable Nietzsche,* trans. and ed. W. Kaufmann (New York: Viking Press, 1968), p. 252. Cf. Heidegger, "Who is Nietzsche's Zarathustra?" in *The New Nietzsche,* ed. D. B. Allison, (New York: Dell, 1977), pp. 70–74.

13. Richard Rorty, *Philosophy and the Mirror of Nature* (Princeton: Princeton University Press, 1979).

14. Ibid., pp. 3–13.

15. Ibid., pp. 315–22, 379–89.

16. Friedrich Nietzsche, *The Gay Science,* trans. W. Kaufmann (New York: Vintage Books, 1974), pp. 181–82.

17. The dialogical relation between God and humans is developed at length in Karl Barth. *Church Dogmatics,* trans. G. W. Bromiley and T. F. Torrance (Edinburgh: T. & T. Clark, 1960) III, 2. Buber comments on his own dialogical principle and compares it with Barth's in Martin Buber, *Between Man and Man,* trans. R. G. Smith (New York: Macmillan, 1965).

18. Both of these points are treated at length by Barth in his Doctrine of Creation. I may say, in passing, that a real reclamation of the radical nature of Barth's thought has barely begun, in the English literature at any rate. Cf. George Hunsinger, ed., *Karl Barth and Radical Politics,* (Philadelphia: Westminster Press, 1976).

19. Karl Marx, *Writings of the Young Marx on Philosophy and Society,* ed. L. D. Easten and K. H. Gaddat (Garden City, N.Y.: Anchor-Doubleday, 1967) and Ludwig Feuerbach, *The Fiery Brook: Selected Writings of Ludwig Feuerbach,* trans. Z. Hanfi (Garden City, N.Y.: Anchor-Doubleday, 1972), contain some of the representative texts on this point.

20. This contradiction in Marx's thought is brought out by a generally overlooked but valuable book by Tillich, Paul Tillich, *The Socialist Decision,* trans. Franklin Sherman (New York: Harper & Row, 1977).

21. Friedrich Nietzsche, *The Will to Power,* trans. W. Kaufmann and R. J. Hollingdale (New York: Vintage Books, 1968), p. 513.

22. This Heideggerian notion is developed in Raschke as the end both in the sense of completion and fulfillment.

23. Martin Heidegger, *Identity and Difference,* trans. J. Stambaugh (New York: Harper & Row, 1969).

24. Harold Bloom, "The Breaking of Form," in *Deconstruction and Criticism* (New York: Seabury Press, 1979) pp. 4–14.

25. Martin Buber in *I and Thou,* trans. R. G. Smith (New York: Scribner's, 1958) and Heidegger, *The Question Concerning Technology and Other Essays.* Both comment on the uncanny as a specific mood engendered in human being by a technological or "it" world which points beyond itself.

26. Heidegger, in *The Question of Being,* trans. J. Wilde and W.

Kluback (New Haven: College and University Press Publishers, 1958), discusses the nature of nihilism in both its senses.

27. Heidegger made this a key point in his early work and retained it, with various modifications, throughout his career of thought.

28. Gadamer; and Jacques Derrida, *Speech and Phenomena,* trans. D. Allison (Evanston: Northwestern University Press, 1973).

29. This is, of course, the moment of negation with which, according to Hegel, all thought begins.

30. Georg Lukács, *History and Class Consciousness,* trans. R. Livingstone (Cambridge: MIT Press, 1971), pp. 116–49. Just as Hegel "ontologised" the antinomies of thought in Kant's sense and overcame them through the absolute philosophy, Lukács "socialized" them and overcame them "proleptically" in the revolution of the proletariat.

31. G. A. Cohen, *Karl Marx's Theory of History: A Defense* (Princeton: Princeton University Press, 1979), pp. 129–33.

32. Jacques Derrida, *Writing and Difference,* trans. A. Bass (Chicago: University of Chicago Press, 1978). Raschke contains an interesting and relevant treatment of Derrida's position.

33. G. W. F. Hegel, *The Science of Logic,* trans. A. V. Miller (London: Allen and Unwin, 1969).

34. Derrida, *Writing and Difference.* Richard Mackey and Eugenio Donato, eds., *The Structuralist Controversy: The Languages of Criticism and the Sciences of Man* (Baltimore: Johns Hopkins Press, 1972), contains an interesting discussion of just this point in Derrida's work.

35. Martin Heidegger, *On the Way to Language,* trans. P. Hertz (New York: Harper & Row, 1971).

36. J. L. Austin, *Philosophical Papers,* ed. J. O. Urmson and G. J. Warnock (Oxford: Oxford University Press, 1970).

37. Jürgen Habermas, *Communication and the Evolution of Society,* trans. T. McCarthy (Boston: Beacon Press, 1979), pp. 65–68.

38. Collingwood, *The Idea of History,* pp. 282–302.

39. Gadamer, *Truth and Method,* pp. 325–41.

40. Habermas, *Knowledge and Human Interests,* pp. 214–73, and *Theory and Practice,* pp. 195–252.

41. R. G. Collingwood, *An Autobiography* (Oxford: Oxford University Press, 1978), pp. 29–43.

42. H. R. Niebuhr, "The Ego-Alter Dialectic and the Conscience," *Journal of Philosophy* 42 (1946), pp. 106–17.

43. John Dewey, *Reconstruction in Philosophy* (Boston: Beacon Press, 1967), discusses his understanding of reconstruction as applied in various realms. Richard Bernstein, *Praxis and Action* (Philadelphia: University of Pennsylvania Press, 1971), brings pragmatism into relation with Existentialism and Marxism.

44. Paul Tillich, *The Courage to Be* (New Haven: Yale University Press, 1961), pp. 182–90.

45. Jean-Paul Sartre, *Being and Nothingness,* trans. H. Barnes (New York: Philosophical Library, 1956). In Sartre's early work, as in Heidegger's, the entire analysis of human being is worked out in terms of a project in the present out of the past into the future. Thus, human being is itself "unmeant" while bestowing meaning on being. Both Sartre and Heidegger, in their later works, turn from this exclusively instrumental approach to the dialogical, though in very different ways.

46. Wilfred Cantwell Smith, *Religious Diversity* (New York: Harper & Row, 1976).

6

THOMAS J. J. ALTIZER

History as Apocalypse

I

Theologically, it would not be amiss to identify the deconstruction movement as a contemporary expression of demythologizing, and particularly so if we were to follow Derrida and conceive "the logos" to be de-constructed or de-centered as God's infinite understanding.[1] Gifted or cursed as we now are with a necessarily, but newly, ahistorical sense, we also no longer know whether the presence of a primordial logos is more or less ancient than the absence of God or being.[2] Derrida's project presumes that "absence" is older than "presence" or history, even if this presumption cannot occur until the end of history, for Derrida believes quite simply and literally that the absolute knowledge realized in modernity is the "*closure* if not the end of history."[3]

> And we believe *that such a closure has taken place*. The history of being as presence, as self-presence in absolute knowledge, as consciousness of self in the infinity of *parousia*—this history is closed. The history of presence is closed, for "history" has never meant anything but the presentation (*Gegenwärtigung*) of Being, the production and recollection of beings in presence, as knowledge and mastery. Since absolute self-presence in con-sciousness is the infinite *vocation* of full presence, the achievement of absolute knowledge is the end of the infinite, which could only be the unity of the concept, logos, and consciousness in a voice without *differance*.[4]

"Voice without *differance*" might well be taken as an Hebraic or Old Testament response to and identification of the Christian symbol of the incarnate Word, even if Derrida has most fundamentally drawn his conceptual understanding of presence, consciousness, and history from Hegel and his primal method or way of deconstruction or decentering from Nietzsche.

If the very word *differance* is a decisive key to Derrida's project, it is also a decisive way into our posthistorical or postmodern world, and most clearly so insofar as it presents itself as belonging to no category of either history or philosophy. As Derrida repeatedly notes, his employment of *differance* is often indiscernible from the movement of negation in negative theology. While Derrida insists that *differance* is not theological, not even in the most negative order of negative theology, it would appear that this is so only in the perspective of a Christian identification of God as pure or immediate presence. *Differance* is, or course, unnameable for this most iconoclastic of our contemporary thinkers, and he maintains that there is nothing kerygmatic about this word so long as we can perceive its reduction to a lower-case letter. Nevertheless, he employs Nietzschean language and says that we must affirm it, and do so with a certain laughter and a certain dance.[5] If our language has no name for such a *differance,* this is because *differance* is "older" than being itself, and therefore is the preprimordial unnameable. There is and can be no name for absolute origin, for pure trace, or for *differance,* not even the name *differance,* for *differance* is not a name, nor does it name the nameless, for it is "older" than the primordial name, the Name of God.

Both in his dialogical responses to Edmond Jabès and in his extraordinarily powerful and self-revealing analysis of the thought of his own mentor, Emmanual Levinas, "Reb Derissa" or Derrida has unveiled his own ground in Lurianic Kabbalism, perhaps the most deeply modern or postmodern of all forms of mystical thinking. Two Lurianic doctrines in particular are related to Derrida's thinking: (1)

on *zimzum* (God's retraction or withdrawal into himself in order to make possible the creation); and (2) on *shevirat ha-kelim* (the "breaking of the vessels"). Derrida can conjoin these themes as follows: "The breaking of the Tables articulates, first of all, a rupture within God as the origin of history."

> God separated himself from himself in order to let us speak, in order to astonish and interrogate us. He did so not by speaking but by keeping still, by letting silence interrupt his voice and his signs, by letting the Tables be broken.[6]

A Kabbalistic vision of God's contraction or self-withdrawal (*zimzum*) is surely one decisive source of Derrida's ground in a groundless beginning, a preprimordial "hole" rather than a primordial plenum, which Derrida can speak of as the "original exile" from the kingdom of being, an exile which signifies that: "Being never is, never shows *itself*, is never *present*, is never *now*, outside difference (in all the senses required by this word)."[7]

Despite the call of the deconstructionist movement to ahistorical thinking, it is simply impossible to imagine Derrida as anything but a twentieth-century thinker, and perhaps the only thinker who has responded as thinker to the Holocaust. Therein it is impossible to dissociate Derrida from the greatest composer of the twentieth century, Arnold Schoenberg, and most especially so since the late Schoenberg became such a profoundly Jewish composer, a move following his reconversion to Judaism in 1933. Above all it is Schoenberg's *Moses and Aaron* which is closest to Derrida, a work which was the culmination of Schoenberg's revolutionary genius, for the entire work rests on a single twelve-tone row and its various transpositions and inversions, as here strict serial unity culminates in an opera after having successfully been realized in piano music, chamber works, and large orchestral works. Schoenberg wrote his own libretto for *Moses and Aaron,* but he never wrote the music for the third

and final act, so all too significantly the opera thereby ends
with Moses' shattering of the Tables of the Law. The opera
itself revolves about a violent and ultimate confrontation
between Moses and Aaron, the older brother and prophet
portrayed as the embodiment of Spirit and the younger as
the embodiment of Word. It is Aaron, the servant of the
Word, who presents the golden calf to the people, a
presentation which culminates in the opera with an orgiastic
dance. Then Moses appears, destroys the calf, and in the
space of two bars the people leave the stage in horror, and
the terrible and decisive confrontation between the
brothers occurs at the end of act two. Moses, in a fit of
impotent rage, destroys the Tables of the Law. Then and
only then do the people return triumphantly, a return
which, however, leads Moses to a solitary despair, a despair
leading to his last monologoue, one of the most powerful
moments in all opera.

> Inconceivable God:
> Inexpressible, many-sided idea,
> will you let it be so explained?
> Shall Aaron, my mouth, fashion this image?
> Then I have fashioned an image too, false,
> as an image must be.
> Thus am I defeated!
> Thus, all was but madness that
> I believed before,
> and can and must not be given voice.
> O word, thou word, that I lack![8]

Thus it is Schoenberg who has given us not only an image
but a full musical realization of the first and greatest of the
prophets as a prophet finally lacking word or logos, and a
prophet who thereby and therein destroys all revelation
which can be given voice.

   Allowing Schoenberg, Kafka, and Derrida to stand for
the Jewish or Hebraic witness in our century, we can see
that it is a radically and purely iconoclastic witness even
while thereby embodying a truly new and comprehensive

purity and unity. Certainly from a Christian perspective, and above all from the horizon of the Christian God and Word, it is a profound and purely negative assault upon faith and revelation, and thus is literally a movement of deconstruction. Here is demythologizing far more radical than that effected by any Christian theologian, and a negative vision transcending that of any gentile thinker or visionary of the twentieth century. Yet just as Philo and Spinoza had a far deeper impact upon the Christian world than upon Judaism, it is not inconceivable that this uniquely modern or postmodern Jewish witness is absolutely necessary and essential to the very survival of Christianity. As Harry Wolfson taught us, it was Philo who made possible and thereby created the whole classical tradition of Christian philosophical theology, and Spinoza who brought that tradition to an end. Is it possible that a uniquely twentieth-century Jewish witness will bring the whole tradition of modern Christianity to an end, and thereby make possible a new Christian beginning?

I I

If Hegel is the supreme thinker of a uniquely modern Christianity, and also the culmination of what Heidegger construes as the onto-theological tradition and Derrida as logocentrism, he is so most clearly in his philosophy or theology of history, wherein history is finally identified as the self-realization or self-embodiment of God. Of course, the distinctively modern method or movement of Hegelian logic is self-negation or pure negativity, a movement culminating historically with the advent of full or pure self-consciousness in the modern world, an advent which is the historical realization of the Incarnation. Therein history presents itself and is manifest for the first time as an integral and comprehensive whole, an organic whole which is a consequence of the negation or self-negation of all preconscious and prehistorical identity. That self-negation actualizes and realizes itself in consciousness, and as consciousness as well, a consciousness and self-consciousness which is historical reality itself. Therein everything whatsoever which has happened in history is now realized and known in consciousness, and fully realized and known in pure self-consciousness, a self-consciousness or pure and total presence which is the self-realization or self-actualization of Spirit or God.

Now it is highly significant that Derrida accepts virtually the whole of this Hegelian understanding of history and consciousness, even if only to effect its total negation, but thereby he is following the path of Nietzsche, and not only Nietzsche but a host of modern thinkers and visionaries as well. All post-Hegelian reverse-Hegelian movements revolve about the postulation or realization of the end of history or the death of God, and here it is of fundamental importance to realize that the end of history and the death of God are not only simultaneous but identical movements. The end of history is the end or self-negation of self-consciousness, an ending which is fully and openly embodied in the twentieth century, and an ending which is eschatological in the sense that it is an absolute end of everything which is here manifest and real as history itself. So it is that the end of history has, indeed, occurred, and not simply the history of metaphysics, but the history of the West as a whole, for the "metaphysical" identification of being as presence is simply the philosophical voice of the Western consciousness itself.

One of Derrida's unique philosophical achievements is to have realized a full conceptual identity of voice, and therein voice makes manifest its theological ground and source:

> God is the name and the element of that which makes possible an absolutely pure and absolutely self-present self-knowledge. From Descartes to Hegel and in spite of all the differences that separate the different places and moments in the structure of that epoch, God's infinite understanding is the other name for the logos as self-presence. The logos can be infinite and self-present, it can be produced as *auto-affection,*

only through the *voice:* an order of the signifier by which the subject takes from itself into itself, does not borrow outside of itself the signifier that it emits and that affects it at the same time. Such is at least the experience—or consciousness—of the voice: of hearing (understanding)-oneself-speak [*s'entendre-parler*].[9]

Derrida understands consciousness in an Hegelian mode as the actual experience of pure auto-affection or self-consciousness, but he goes beyond Hegel not only by associating consciousness and voice but by identifying consciousness and voice, thereby making possible an understanding of the experience of voice as the exclusion of all exterior, sensible, and spatial sources of self-presence.

At bottom God or logos is the source and ground of the exclusion or negation of all alien sources of self-presence, and is so precisely because God is total presence, a presence which negates and excludes everything which cannot become present, and which cannot become present in consciousness or history. Derrida is dedicated to resurrecting that excluded or negated absence, even if such a resurrection can never be effected in history, consciousness, or language, and cannot be so effected if only because the irreversible event of God's total self-presence has already occurred. Ironically, it is Kafka, Schoenberg, and Derrida who embody the most compelling witness to the Incarnation in our world. For all of them in their fullest and purest work embody worlds of meaning and identity which are absolutely free of any ground or source outside themselves. Nevertheless, their worlds echo or reflect an emptiness outside of themselves. That emptiness is a pure emptiness, not in the Buddhist sense, but rather in a fully western sense, for it is an emptiness which actually affects consciousness, even if it thereby profoundly dislodges consciousness from its given center and ground.

Indeed, Derrida's Hegelian conception of logos or presence is at once a conception of a totally incarnate Word and a universal or catholic word which is the ultimate source and ground of all actual meaning and identity. So it is that it is against this very background and foreground of the totality and universality of presence or logos that Derrida establishes his impossible project of recovering that "trace" which is sublimated and erased in pure and total presence. True, this project is made possible by the end of history or the death of God, but it remains an impossible project, and is so because of the total and ineradicable effects of the very actualization of a total presence. A metaphysical era that began in Platonism and ended in infinitist metaphysics succeeded in wholly reducing or dissolving the "difference" in presence, thereby wholly sublimating the "trace," and, as Derrida says, "the logos as the sublimation of the trace is *theological*."[10] Only the pure and total presence of a total and positive infinity could dissolve all real or actual difference, but that dissolution has manifestly occurred, as *differance* remains unspeakable. Upon reflection, one wonders if it would be possible to be more Hegelian than Derrida; or, more Hegelian in a post-Hegelian or posthistorical age.

Just as Derrida most openly unveils his philosophical identity in the depth of his response to the truly anti-Hegelian Levinas, and perhaps most significantly remains an Hegelian in his very refusal of Levinas's infinitely other God,[11] so Derrida most clearly reveals his human identity in response to the profoundly theological poetic language of Jabès. In Derrida's Hegelian mood, grace is that which is most missing, but the presence of the poet, whether Artaud or Jabès, seems to make Derrida dance, and to dance by way of a Godless play.

Just as there is a negative theology, there is a negative atheology. An accomplice of the former, it still pronounces the absence of a center, when it is play that should be affirmed. But is not the desire for a center, as a function of play itself, the indestructable itself? And in the repetition or return of play, how could the phantom of the center not call to us? It is here that the hesitation between writing as decentering and writing as an affirmation of play is infinite. This hesitation is part of play and links it to death.[12]

Alas, a fully Godless or pagan play is closed to Derrida, as is innocence itself, for the desire for a center is not only indestructible but is the indestructible itself. Even play is an expression of that desire, for God is truly inescapable.

III

God is the name of that center which is everywhere, but it is everywhere only by being nowhere where it is only itself, and therefore nowhere in the absence or silence of consciousness or speech. That is the nowhere which is the goal of Derrida's project, a goal which he names as writing or the Book, for what disappears in writing is the self-identity of the origin, the self-presence of living speech.[13] Derrida is the one in our time who has most fully recovered or restored the purely iconoclastic identity of the Book, and therewith the purely aniconic identity of pure writing or trace. That trace is the concealment of the origin, a concealment which is the unnameable movement of *difference-itself*, which Derrida strategically "nicknames" *differance*, and which can be called writing only within the *historical* closure of absolute knowledge.[14] So it is that it is the death of God which makes possible the return of *difference-itself*, a pure difference which is lost with the advent of history or consciousness, and a difference or *differance* which is the true "other" of God. That which could be known by both a metaphysical and a biblical theology as the Nihil can be known by a "new" Kabbalah as the absolutely unnameable, and absolutely unnameable because it is "older" than language.

In the perspective of the project of Derrida, there is and can be no true writing, no true representation or embodiment of any kind. And this is so not simply because truth is inseparable from presence, and thus is the erasure or sublimation of trace, but also because truth only appears through the exteriority of writing, an exteriority marking an uncrossable distance between the signified and the signifier. Inasmuch as deconstruction is a demolition of all the significations that have their source in the logos, it is most particularly so a destruction of the signification of truth.[15] Once again deconstruction is only possible through the end of history or the death of God, an end which makes possible the discovery of "writing" or the trace. Remarkably enough, however, it thereby makes possible a rediscovery or new discovery of history and presence, and of history as presence, as full or total presence. Only in the perspective of the rebirth of trace does history fully reveal itself as total presence, for only then does history actually appear as the erasure or sublimation of *difference-itself,* a difference which cannot appear within the horizon of history itself. Thus it is the manifestation of *difference-itself,* a manifestation made possible only by the end of history, which unveils the apocalyptic identity of history as total presence.

Surely one of the most distinctive signs of a seemingly posthistorical era is the erosion or erasure of the meaning and identity of history itself. History can appear to us either as a totality embracing all meaning and identity or as a night in which no distinctions remain and are real. And finally nothing distinguishes such a totality from such a night! Or, rather, that which distinguishes them is an unnameable difference, a difference marked by the silence of speech and the absence of God, a silence of speech which is the absence of God. Just as the presence of speech inevitably bears an imprint or a sign of its origin in a center or logos, so absence or the absence of speech is always a distancing from God.[16] Pure silence or pure trace is at a total distance from God, but it is just this distance which unveils the total presence of God in the pure sublimation of trace. History is that sublimation or erasure, and in the presence of history *difference-itself* is absent, and is absent by virtue of an absolute or total presence. This is the meaning or identity of history that dawns with the end of history or the death of God, and ironically enough it is an identity or meaning which is even more total or absolute than is the meaning of history prior to that end.

Heidegger and Derrida, following Hegel and Nietzsche, have shown us how a metaphysics of being *as* being inevitably and necessarily passed into and realized itself as a metaphysics of presence, a presence which is the totality of history or consciousness. In this perspective, there is and can be no final or ultimate theological distinction between creation and history, or cosmos and consciousness, and cannot be because creation and history are only limited and finite names of the realization and embodiment of an absolute and total or infinite presence. If only for purposes of identification, we might say that ontological being and cosmological being are signs of classical Christianity, just as fully or wholly self-conscious Spirit and absolute history are signs of modern Christianity. Just as modern Christianity evolved out of classical Christianity, so classical Christianity is the matrix and seed of modern Christianity. It was not for nothing that Heidegger was driven to recover a pre-Platonic logos, just as Derrida even more radically is driven to seek a prehistorical or ahistorical trace, for everything which is manifest and real as history to us bears the imprint or the sign not only of an occidental being but also of the Christian God. Yet it is only in the wake of the death of the Christian God that the omnipresence of God becomes overwhelmingly manifest.

Even as Christianity is so profoundly grounded in a Pauline dialectic of guilt and grace and a Johannine dialectic of darkness and light, so in our world it is the death of God that has irrevocably and irreversibly made manifest and real the omnipresence of God, an omnipresence that is indistinguishable from consciousness and speech. Of course, it is at this very point that consciousness and speech themselves are most profoundly in question, and in question in terms of their very existence and identity. It might even be said that it is just the new nameability of the omnipresence of God that realizes or actualizes the new unnameability of consciousness and speech. For the unnameability which Derrida finds in *differance* is now found at the frontiers of language and speech, as the end of history realizes itself in a hole in consciousness and an absence or emptiness or dissonance of speech. If our beginning is marked by a grounding in a center or a naming of God, our end is marked by a rebirth or renewal of centerlessness which is, nevertheless, precisely thereby a realization not of the Name of God but rather of the omnipresence of God, an omnipresence which erodes and disrupts all language and speech. So it is that the omnipresence of God cannot be spoken or named as such, or, rather, it can be named and spoken only as the death of God.

The naming of "God," as Robert P. Scharlemann has shown, is the ending of the pure identity of God as God, of God as pure transcendence. Thus the naming of God exiles God from God: "God becomes manifest in language not as such but as other than God and thus as in exile from deity."[17] Accordingly, the God who is manifest and real in history and consciousness is not "God," not the God of pure transcendence. This a Christian motif at least as old as Meister Eckhart, and perhaps historically as old as Yahwism itself, and it might be said to mark the deepest response of both Judaism and Islam to Christianity. Theologically, this motif was decisively reborn in Luther's purely negative identification of the God of law and judgment, and then reborn systematically and conceptually in Kierkegaard's dialectical and comprehensive understanding of the God of objective thinking and historical Christendom as the opposite of the God of faith, and then reborn in multiple forms in the Protestant dialectical theology of the twentieth century. But perhaps its most poignant and compelling expression in our time lies present in the work of Mircea Eliade. As Eliade notes in his journal:

> Today when I was leafing through my *Patterns in Comparative Religion,* I lingered especially over the long chapter on the sky gods; I wonder if the secret message of the book has been

understood, the "theology" implied in the history of religions as I decipher and interpret it. And yet the meaning emerges clearly: myths and religions, in all their variety, are the results of the vacuum left in the world by the retreat of God, his transformation into *deus otiosus,* and his disappearance from the religious scene. God—or, more precisely, the Supreme Being—no longer played an active role in the religious experience of primitive humanity. He was supplanted by other divine forms—divinities which were active, fertile, dramatic, etc. I returned to the subject of this process in other studies. But has it been understood that "true" religion begins only after God has withdrawn from the world? That his transcendence merges and coincides with his eclipse?[18]

Nowhere else has Eliade more fully revealed his theological identity, and this identity might be seen as underlying a uniquely modern understanding of religion as religion. Or, as Eliade can straightforwardly declare:

Religion is indeed the result of "the fall," "the forgetting," the loss of the state of primordial perfection. In paradise, Adam knew nothing of religious experience, nor of theology, that is, the doctrine of God. Before "sin," *there was no religion.*[19]

In this perspective we can see that the death of God could make possible a return or resurrection of the original or purely transcendent identity of God as God. Thereby the disappearance of God from consciousness and history could be understood as precisely the way by which the original identity of God could become manifest. And remarkably enough it is thereby and only thereby that the total omnipresence of God becomes manifest and real. Of course, it is not possible for us to name that omnipresence as the omnipresence of "God." We can only know that omnipresence as the death of God, as the total disappearance of God from consciousness and history, as the disappearance and dissolution of everything which we have named and known as God. So it is that the death of

God appears hand in hand with the reappearance or resurrection of a pure trace which is the opposite of God. Indeed, the very namelessness of that trace is a decisive sign of its integral relation with the namelessness of God, for both are absolutely and totally unnameable, an unnameability which places them at an absolute distance from everything which we have known as language, consciousness, and history. But the appearance of that unnameability nevertheless names our history, and it names it as the absolute sublimation of trace, which is simultaneously the total presence of God.

IV

Now what can be the relation between what Derrida names as trace and what the Christian names or has named as God? While both present themselves as being immediately self-evident in their meaning and identity, upon reflection both soon lose that self-evident identity, and so much so that neither can then remain what it initially appeared to mean or to be. Derrida would teach us that trace is virtually invisible in the fullness of history or presence, and a posthistorical age has discovered that God is no longer either nameable or speakable. If an imprint of trace is born or reborn in the twentieth century, that birth is certainly not confined to the work of Derrida, and we may find an earlier correlate of trace in Sartre's philosophical category of *de trop* or "too much." *De trop* for Sartre is pure contingency and it is the essence of human existence in its relation to a totally meaningless and Godless world. Pure contingency in this radically modern or postmodern sense reverses the medieval scholastic meaning of contingency, for so far from being an indisputable sign of the necessary existence and presence of God, it now becomes an undeniable sign of the total absence or nonexistence of God. This reversal is, of course, a consequence of the death of God, but even as a classical Christianity could know contingency as a sign of a beneficent creator, so a posthistorical world can know contingency as offering the possibility of a total liberation or redemption.

Sartre introduces his category of *de trop* in his first and most important novel, *Nausea,* which revolves about a primal experience of nausea produced by man's naked encounter with the world, an experience of deep revulsion against the sheer *isness* of the world. Antoine Roquentin, the diarist who is the hero or antihero of the novel, has a dread of touching objects, for the actual presence of objects consumes the center or subject of consciousness. Full nausea unveils the inescapable reality of *de trop,* a pure contingency in which we are both nowhere and unwanted, and therein we inescapably realize that we are *de trop* for eternity. And the experience of nausea brings Roquentin not the idea, but the actual feeling, of the absurdity of existence: "And without formulating anything clearly, I understood that I had found the key to Existence, the key to my Nauseas, to my own life."[20]

> This moment was extraordinary. I was there, motionless and icy, plunged in a horrible ecstasy. But something fresh had just appeared in the very heart of this ecstasy: I understood the Nausea, I possessed it. To tell the truth, I did not formulate my discoveries to myself. But I think it would be easy for me to put them in words now. The essential thing is contingency. I mean that one cannot define existence as necessity. To exist is simply *to be there.* . . . No necessary being can explain existence: contingency is not a delusion, a probability which can be dissipated; it is the absolute, consequently, the perfect free gift.[21]

Sartre tries but fails in this novel to create an acceptance of nausea, and, indeed, he never later succeeded in unveiling the meaning of pure contingency as absolute grace.

Nevertheless, it is possible to say that the greatest works of art of the twentieth century reveal pure contingency as absolute grace. Surely this is so, and fundamentally so, of the novel which most deeply shaped the modern French mind, Proust's *A la recherche du temps perdu*. This is a quest for lost time which at bottom is a quest for redemption or eternity, and even as it succeeds in plumbing the depths of each of the characters which it explores, that depth finally becomes manifest as a pure contingency or anonymity of consciousness, yet it is precisely therein that pure time or eternity is recaptured. Proust presents a concrete analysis of this movement of redemption in *Le temps retrouvé,* the final volume of the novel, which there is now good reason to believe was conceived before any other portion of the work. At midpoint in this volume, an unexpected movement occurs, when the narrator, thoroughly disillusioned with life, is about to enter a reception at the mansion of the Princess de Guermantes (a new Guermantes who is a vulgar reversal of all those noble qualities of the Guermantes family which had earlier excited the veneration of the narrator). Now the narrator accidentally trips against the uneven paving stones in front of the coach house, and immediately all his discouragement vanishes and in its place is that same happiness which at various points in his life had been given him: "But it is sometimes just at the moment when we think that everything is lost that the intimation arrives which may save us; one knocks at all the doors which lead nowhere, and then one stumbles without knowing it on the only door which one can enter—which one might have sought in vain for a hundred years—and it opens of its own accord."[22]

Here, stumbling is a fully appropriate image, for the action which induces the ecstatic moment of happiness is wholly accidental, and when the narrator merely repeats the physical movement nothing is achieved. Despite his inclination to remain outside, the narrator enters the Guermantes mansion, and while waiting in a little sitting room used as a library, a second intimation comes to reinforce the first, this one occassioned by a servant accidentally knocking a spoon against a plate. Once again he is ecstatically carried into the past, and then within seconds, he wipes his mouth with a napkin, and the ecstatic experience occurs once more:

> . . . a new vision of azure passed before my eyes, but an azure that this time was pure and saline and swelled into blue and bosomy undulations, and so strong was this impression that the moment to which I was transported seemed to me to be the present moment: more bemused than on the day when I asked myself whether I were really going to be received by the Princess de Guermantes or whether everything round me would not collapse, I thought that the servant had just opened the window unto the beach and that all things invited me to go down and stroll along the promenade while the tide was high, for the napkin which I had used to wipe my mouth had precisely the same degree of stiffness as the towel with which I found it so awkward to dry my face as I stood in front of the window on the very first day of my arrival at Balbec and this napkin now, in the library of the Prince de Guermantes' house, unfolded for me—concealed within its smooth surface and its folds—the plumage of an ocean green and blue like the tail of a peacock. And what I found myself enjoying was not merely these colors but a whole instant of my life on whose summit they rested, an instant which had been no doubt an aspiration towards them and which some feeling of fatigue or sadness had perhaps prevented me from enjoying at Balbec but which now, freed from what is necessarily imperfect in external perception, pure and disincarnate, caused me to swell with happiness.[23]

He had known such experiences before, while a child at Combray in tasting the little *madeleine,* and much later, while standing upon two uneven stones in the baptistry of St. Mark's in Venice; but never before with such intensity. And only now, at the end of the novel, does he realize their meaning.

Proust notes that the ecstatic moment is experienced in the present moment and at the same time in the context of a distant moment, so that the past encroaches upon the present in such a manner as to make it indistinguishable from the present. But Proust asks if this moment of the past is not perhaps something very much more essential than either the present or the past:

> So often, in the course of my life, reality had disappointed me because at the instant when my senses perceived it my imagination, which was the only organ I possessed for the enjoyment of beauty, could not apply itself to it, in virtue of that ineluctable law which ordains that we can only imagine what is absent. And now, suddenly, the effect of this harsh law had been neutralized, temporarily annulled, by a marvellous expedient of nature which had caused a sensation—the noise made both by the spoon and by the hammer, for instance—to be mirrored at one and the same time in the past, so that my imagination was permitted to savor it, and in the present, where the actual shock to my senses of the noise, the touch of the linen napkin, or whatever it might be, had added to the dream of the imagination the concept of "existence" which they usually lack, and through this subterfuge had made it possible for my being to secure, to isolate, to immobilize—for a moment brief as a flash of lightning—what normally it never apprehends, a fragment of time in the pure state.[24]

So it is that if a sensation once experienced in the past is experienced again in the present and at the same time in the past, "real" without being actual, "ideal" without being abstract, then immediately our "true self" is awakened as if from the dead: "A minute freed from the order of time has re-created in us, to feel it, the man freed from the order of time."[25] This ultimate freedom or transcendence is situated outside of time, or outside the vicissitudes of time, and yet it is in some sense a moment of past time:

> . . . the slightest word that we have said, the most insignificant action that we have performed at any one epoch of our life was surrounded by, and colored by the reflection of, things which logically had no connection with it and which later have been separated from it by our intellect which could make nothing of them for its own rational purposes, things,

however, in the midst of which . . . the simplest act or gesture remains immured as within a thousand sealed vessels, each of them filled with things of a color, a scent, a temperature that are absolutely different one from another. . . . Yes: if, owing to the work of oblivion, the returning memory can throw no bridge, form no connecting link between itself and the present minute, if it remains in the context of its own place and date, if it keeps its distance, its isolation in the hollow of a valley or upon the highest peak of a mountain summit, for this very reason it causes us suddenly to breathe a new air, an air which is new precisely because we breathed it in the past, that purer air which the poets have vainly tried to situate in paradise and which could induce so profound a sense of renewal only if it had been breathed before, since the true paradises are the paradises which we have lost.[26]

In this, the best-known of all passages in Proust's work, we discover that it is the work of *oblivion* which isolates a concrete moment of past time and thus makes possible its preservation in a pure state. This wholly isolated moment of time can only be released in the present by an accidental and unforeseen experience, an experience reenacting or re-presenting the concretion and contingency of the initial or original moment of a now isolated and pure time. And it is precisely the concrescence of the immediacy and actuality of the initial moment with the purity and timelessness of its wholly isolated form which is the source of the Proustian ecstasy. Here, we find a genuine *coincidentia oppositorum,* a full coming together of the naked immediacy of a concrete moment of time with its own inherent opposite, with a pure and disincarnate moment. Yet it is the same moment of time which is simultaneously "real" and "ideal," real in the sense that it once actually occurred in the present, and ideal in the sense that the work of oblivion has wholly isolated it from the actuality of the concrete present. It is just this inherent opposition of the "real" and "ideal" poles of a moment of full time which makes necessary the purely accidental and contingent nature of the experience which releases this moment in the present. As Proust insists so eloquently, the purer air which induces so profound a sense of renewal is an air which we have breathed before, and it is a "new air" which is new precisely because we breathed it in the past. If the Proustian moment is primordial, it is not a prehistoric mythical moment of the beginning, *ab origine,* but rather a moment which was actually lived in the concrete and profane time of duration. True, the work of oblivion annuls the contingency of that moment, but the purity achieved by this work of interior isolation can become incarnate or real only when it is conjoined with the immediacy of concrete time.

We must not view the Prousian renewal or repetition of lost time in isolation, but rather understand it as a paradigmatic gesture for us, a gesture which is repeated in innumerable modes throughout the body of our greatest twentieth-century art, music, and literature. A pure repetition of this gesture, purer by far than Proust's, is embodied in Rilke's celebration of *einmal* in the Ninth Elegy:

> *Einmal*
> *jedes, nur einmal. Einmal und nicht mehr. Und wir auch*
> *einmal. Nie wieder. Aber dieses*
> *einmal gewessen zu sein, wenn auch nur einmal:*
> *irdisch gewessen zu sein, scheint nicht widerrufbar.*

> Just once,
> everything only for once. Once and no more. And we, too,
> Once, and never again, but this
> having been once, though only once,
> having been once on earth—can it ever be cancelled?

This ecstatic affirmation comes as an answer to the poet's question: why must we be human? And it culminates in Rilke's apocalyptic vision of the resurrection of the earth invisibly within us, but not before it has enacted the primal act of naming or saying, a praising which names only what is sayable to us:

Hier ist des Säglichen Zeit, hier seine Heimat.
Sprich und bekenn. Mehr als je
fallen die Dinge dahin, die erlebbaren, denn,
was sie verdrängend ersetz, ist Tun ohne Bild.

Here is the time for the Tellable, *here* is its home.
Speak and proclaim. More than ever
the things we can live with are falling away, and their place
being oustingly taken up by an imageless act.[28]

This *here* and *now* concerns us, us the most transient of
beings, for our *einmal* can never be cancelled precisely
because it is a "once and no more." Earth is our ultimate
destiny, and it is by wholly living *here* and *now* that death
itself becomes friendly, and an infinite or transcendent but
totally present existence (*Überzahliges Dasein*) rises in our
heart.

Rilke's triumphant affirmation of *einmal* embodies a
wholly and totally human act of naming, a praising of our
destiny the earth, and this "once and for all" releases a
uniquely present form of transcendence. Here is the
Säglichen Zeit, the time for our speech and affirmation, but
it is a time when things which we can experience are falling
away from us. For that earth which is our destiny, our home
in the *here* and *now,* is ever more overwhelmingly being
absorbed by an "imageless act." Rilke's imageless act is yet
another paradigmatic sign of a uniquely modern or
postmodern pure contingency, and, it, too, releases or
makes possible yet another apocalyptic vision of an
immediate eternity or resurrection. "Once and no more,"
this ultimate affirmation of the *here* and *now* as our destiny
makes possible a transformation of history, a liberation of
human existence or destiny from its fleetingness, its evasion
of the finality of the concrete and total moment. Those
things, which Rilke apprehends as falling away from us, and
which he praisefully names in the very context of their
absence, might well be compared with those things which
Proust understands as being immediately embedded in our
experience but which logically have no connection with it.

For Proust, these things become interiorly isolated in our memory by the work of oblivion, but they can be awakened or resurrected by a concrete and external event which accidentally reproduces or repeats them, thereby inducing the advent of a totally present eternity. Rilke's naming might also be understood as a repetition of things, and a repetition which says them: "Just once, everything only for once, once and no more." This *einmal* has the finality of apocalypse, and an apocalypse occurring only at the end of history, only at the end or dissolution of that absolute necessity which the Christian has known as God.

V

Just what can it mean to affirm that the end of history has occurred? First, we must note that this is not simply a new or postmodern affirmation, for something very like it lies at the center of the New Testament, even if that center was dislodged and transformed by the historical development and evolution of Christianity. That original Christian center was continually reborn in Christian history, as witness the fullest and most radical expressions of Christian mysticism and Christian apocalypticism. And remarkably enough the very advent of the modern world embodied a comprehensive rebirth of apocalypticism, an apocalypticism extending from romantic poetry to dialectical and idealistic philosophy to revolutionary politics and political action. If we accept Hegel as the primal thinker of modernity, then we can see that apocalypticism and a pure or full historical consciousness go hand in hand, for the full realization of the historical consciousness brings the ancient or premodern world to an end. That historical consciousness in its fullest realization is an absolute or total consciousness, and it can also be named and known as pure self-consciousness, a self-consciousness which is its own creator or ground. Not until Nietzsche's ecstatic discovery of Eternal Recurrence did a pure or total consciousness fully appear as its own ground and source, but that discovery was an interior consummation of nineteenth-century vision and thinking, and it continues to lie before us as perhaps the clearest and most powerful symbolic unveiling of our own interior depths.

Already Hegel conceived the purely inner world as the content of modern art, wherein inwardness shows itself outwardly, yet in such a manner as to triumph over the external by reducing it to relative insignificance. But the Hegel who believed that infinite subjectivity is now the sole habitat of Absolute Spirit is also the Hegel who was persuaded that art no longer counts for us as the highest manner in which truth can realize its existence. No doubt this judgment can no longer stand in the twentieth century, and not only because of the triumphs of twentieth-century art but also and even more deeply because those very triumphs embody a dissolution of self-consciousness in an historically postmodern world. But that dissolution or self-dissolution of self-consciousness is inevitably accompanied by the end of the historical consciousness, and that ending can only be known and realized in consciousness as the end of history itself, the end of the world and actuality of the autonomously existing and acting subject and center of consciousness.

Even if this conception of the end of history is present in Hegel's philosophy of history, and surely present in his logic, it is not fully present, not totally present, as witness the fact that Hegelian language is so comprehensively bound to an interior subjectivity and self-consciousness. Hegel did not live to read the second part of *Faust* or the mature poetry of Hölderlin, nor to encounter his own thinking in a reverse and inverted form in Kierkegaard and Marx, nor to encounter a full expression of that reversal in Nietzsche and late nineteenth-century art and literature. In all of these areas and others pure subjectivity or self-consciousness finally realized itself by ending itself, by ending itself as either a "subject" or "center" of consciousness. Thereafter history could no longer appear and be real as the actualization and realization of an interior subject of consciousness, as interiority fully passed into exteriority, and a new totality is ever more progressively establishing itself which transcends and leaves behind all subjective interiority. Therewith perishes all distinctions between cosmos and consciousness, or selfhood and nature, or nature and history. If an autonomous or self-enclosed nature or world comes to an end with the birth of modern physics, that ending can itself be seen as yet another expression of the end of history, the end of any identity which stands forth and is real by virtue of its own individual presence and actuality.

So it is that the end of history is the death of God, the death of the primal ground of individual presence and actuality, the end or dissolution of the grounding source of all integral and inherent differentiation. Nietzsche's madman asks if there is still any up or down? For now we are continually plunging backward, sideward, forward, and in all directions. That night or infinite nothing into which we have strayed could mythically be named as the chaos prior to the creation. And that is just the reason, mythically considered, why it is no longer possible for us to name God. Nor, of course, can we name ourselves, or name anything whatsoever which is an individual and distinct identity. Yet just as our night is in no sense at all a rebirth of an original innocence, neither is it an impassive or impotent darkness, as witness the incredible power and creativity of modern science and technology. Ours is a darkness of ravaging power, a power without limits, hence the appropriateness of Nietzsche's Dionysian language to name that darkness. However, one of the decisive sources of Nietzsche's Dionysian language is Hegel's *Phenomenology,* and it is significant that Hegel employs the name of Dionysus or Bacchus when he speaks mythically of the power of the negative, as in his most famous aphorism: "The True is thus the Bacchanalian revel in which no member is not drunk."[29]

If the deeper reaches of our darkness embody a Bacchanalian festival, they do so above all in their sheer and total presence, a presence which is not fully or comprehensively realized until the twentieth century. While that presence can now only be actually known or experienced as absence, it is a full presence nonetheless, and is so if only by virtue of the fact that it is actually experienced and known. What Derrida has named as *differance* is present in innumerable forms in twentieth-century science and art. Nothing else is so distinctive of our century, nor is anything of greater significance to us than the sheer fact of this occurrence. Simple identity is what has truly become absent to us, and simple or given identity in all its forms, whether these be subject and object, or matter and spirit, or society and selfhood, or knower and known, no identity whatsoever can any longer stand forth which is only itself. But it is precisely thereby that a total and comprehensive identity is being born in our midst, and that identity is real, as real as modern science and technology, and as modern art, music, and literature, to say nothing of the social and political revolutions of the twentieth century. And it is just because this is a total identity that we can no longer realize it as an historical identity.

Yet if we can no longer know our identity as an historical identity, this very loss of identity can bring a new identity to history itself, and this because we know all too well that our identity is a consequence of historical actuality. If the owl of Minerva flies only with the falling of the dusk, it flies nonetheless, and the very perspective of our night can make possible a new unveiling of a history which has now come to an end. For our darkness is the consummation of history, or the consummation of what can appear and be real to us as history, and thereby history itself passes into a new totality. Now it has always been true that history gains a new identity only as a consequence of the loss of a previous historical identity, and if the end of history has now occurred, that ending could make possible for the first time a total identity of history. Nietzsche's vision of Eternal Recurrence brings such an identity to history, and it was made possible by Nietzsche's historical realization that the totality of consciousness is a consequence of the pure

172 DECONSTRUCTION AND THEOLOGY

negativity of No-saying or the bad conscience. It is just this historical ground which sets this all too modern or postmodern vision of Eternal Recurrence worlds apart from its premodern counterparts, and it is also its historical ground which makes Nietzsche's language and vision so overwhelmingly real to us.

If Nietzsche was himself destroyed by an ultimate and tragic conflict with a uniquely modern nihilism, that nihilism itself thereafter realized both a universal and an historical expression, and an historical expression giving birth to the twentieth century. How ironic that it was the ecstatic prophet of Eternal Recurrence who first philosophically unveiled the total presence of history, a presence possible only by way of the end of history, or the end of every positive meaning and identity of history. Now we can see that Hegel lived too soon to realize such a totally negative identity of history, even if that identity is both logically and historically present in his own comprehension of pure negativity, for a total negativity can only be real as a consequence of a full and total reversal of consciousness. While such a reversal has its counterpart in an Eastern and Buddhist emptying of consciousness, a pure and total negativity is radically different from a pure emptiness if only because it is actually and immediately present, indeed, historically and irreversibly present, and it is just that final and irreversible presence which brings history to an end.

Nothing so characterizes the actuality which we know as its sheer irreversibility, for the first time past time is wholly lost to consciousness, or lost as a living and a human time, and the nostalgia which we know can never be for an earlier history, but only for a prehistorical and primordial plenum. Derrida is but one of a number of our thinkers who have been obsessed with such nostalgia, but all of them know, and Derrida most clearly and decisively, that this is a hopeless and unrealizable nostalgia, and is so perhaps above all when its goal is named not as a plenum but as an absolute emptiness. For that emptiness is truly and actually possible for no one who is a product of a Western history and consciousness, and it is all too significant that Freud himself named the death instinct as the nirvana principle. The innocent among us may well delight in nostalgic fantasy, but not since Shakespeare has an innocent fantasy passed into poetic language, and from Milton through Proust the only paradise which we have known poetically is a paradise lost. Or, rather, the paradise regained in modern art and poetry is not and cannot be an original paradise. Goethe's Faust may finally be redeemed by union with the Eternal Female, just as Blake's Albion may be redeemed by union with Jerusalem, but the redemptive realm of the Mothers and of Jerusalem is as far removed as possible from the original bliss of a Garden of Eden. But perhaps most significant of all, the paradise which has been named by such fully modern poets as Mallarmé and Yeats, is a paradise which is nameable precisely because it does not and cannot exist.

If the advent of the postmodern world embodies a final and eschatological end of history, then history itself can then appear and be real as paradise just because it no longer exists. For it is the loss of a human time and consciousness, and its final and irretrievable loss, which makes possible the discovery of the totality of lost time, a totality which can only mythically and poetically be named as paradise. True, such a paradise could only be an absent, an empty, or a negative paradise, the very paradise which Kafka poetically and parabolically evoked. But this is the only paradise which has ever actually been present upon our horizon, and it is that paradise which released the actuality and irreversibility of history, an irreversibility culminating in the end of history itself. But is there anything else which we can know and name as grace? For the first time we have been given a grace which is everywhere in history, but it is everywhere in history only when history comes to an end, only when history is no longer actual and real.

Now we can follow Nietzsche's madman and say our *requiem aeternam deo,* our requiem to the God who mercifully no longer exists. That requiem and it alone is our way of knowing the omnipresence of God, an omnipresence which appears and is real only with the dissolution and disappearance of its center. History perishes in that dissolution, but that very perishing unveils the final and ultimate identity of history, an apocalyptic identity which is finally no less and no more than the self-embodiment of God. Such an apocalyptic omnipresence of God in history can never be manifest or real as such so long as history itself remains real, only the end of history can unveil the apocalypse of God. And that apocalypse is inseparable from the end or death of God, the death of the God who is only God, the God who can be named and known as God. Only the eschatological and apocalyptic death or dissolution of the God who is God can unveil the omnipresence of God, and the omnipresence of God in history, an omnipresence which can only occur when history is released as an irreversible actuality, and an omnipresence which can only be manifest as an omnipresence of grace when history itself comes to an end. For only when history comes to an end can history be known as grace, just as the only God who can be known as a totally gracious God is the God who is dead.

Christianity has always known the death of God as the way of absolute grace, for nothing less than the death of God lies behind the symbol of the crucifixion, but not until the birth of the modern world is the death of God fully realized in consciousness and history, a realization which is consummated in an absolute or eschatological explosion of history and consciousness. Now grace is everywhere because it is nowhere, nowhere that is where it is only itself, or where it can be known and named as the grace of God. That absolute necessity or *causa sui* which is the classical Christian identity of God has now passed into the center of the world, and that passage has brought the world to an end, or brought an end to every identity which stands forth only as itself. Such an ending is a fully apocalyptic *parousia* or total presence, and therefore it cannot be known as the presence of God, or even as the omnipresence of God, but only as the death of God, the eschatological end of the God who is God. If the naming of God lies at the very origin of our history, and is the original ground of everything which appears and is real to us as integral and individual identity, then the disintegration and disappearance of individual identity is inseparable from the disappearance and end of everything which we have known and named as God. And that is an apocalyptic and eschatological end, a final and total end, and therefore an end which can only be named by the Christian as the realization of absolute grace.

Yes, history is an absolute presence, and the absolute presence of God, but we can only realize such an absolute or totally gracious identity of history when both God and history finally come to an end. And history comes to an end in and as the death of God, the end of the infinite, and therewith the end of all finitude and limits. An absolute and total nihilism is an inevitable consequence of the end of history or the death of God, and this is a nihilism which historically first appears in Christianity, and as early as Paul. Perhaps nothing is more characteristic of primitive Christianity than its ultimate violation of that which Israel absolutely condemned and condemns, the human pronunciation of the Name of God, a pronunciation which a purely iconoclastic faith must judge to be an absolute assault upon the majesty of the creator. At no point did Jesus more radically assault the guardians of an iconoclastic Law or Torah than in commonly addressing God as Abba or "my father," and this is something new in history, for there is no instance of God being addressed as Abba in the literature of Jewish prayer. Indeed, the Pauline Christ redeems the world from the "curse" of the Torah (Galatians 3:13), a Torah which for Paul was ordained not by God but by the angels, and which at best is a tutoring slave (*paidagogos*) to bring the world to Christ. Freedom in Christ, for either Paul or John, is freedom from the Law, a freedom which was reborn again and again in Christian mysticism and apocalypticism, and which decisively and comprehensively entered Western history in the Protestant Reformation. This is a freedom that was a primal source of what we have known as consciousness and history, and a freedom which finally released itself in the ultimate act of deicide, the murder of the creator and judge.

Hegel could know that deicide as the consummation of the Incarnation, an Incarnation which realized the birth of self-consciousness, a self-consciousness which itself becomes absolute by passing through the death of God. With Nietzsche the willing of the death of God becomes the realization of absolute freedom, the creative transformation of the dreadful accident of "it was" into the destiny of "but thus I willed it," as the majesty of the transcendent creator passes into an all too immanent will to power. Thereby a pure nihilism is released in history, and not simply released in history, but consummated in history, a consummation which brings history to an end. Derrida, as every Jewish theological thinker, can recognize this nihilism as a Christian nihilism, a nihilism which is the inevitable consequence of the absolute presence of the Christian God. History is the eschatological embodiment of that God, a God who becomes absolutely present in the Incarnation, an incarnate or self-conscious presence which releases the finality and irreversibility of history. That finality and irreversibility is actuality itself, an actuality which is undeniable and irresistible, and an actuality which is the kenotic emptying of everything which it enacts.

NOTES

1. Jacques Derrida, *Of Grammatology,* trans. Gayatri Chakravorty Spivak (Baltimore: Johns Hopkins University Press, 1976), p. 11.

2. Jacques Derrida, *Speech and Phenomena,* trans. David B. Allison (Evanston: Northwestern University Press, 1973), p. 103.

3. *Speech and Phenomena,* p. 102.

4. *Speech and Phenomena,* p. 102.

5. *Speech and Phenomena,* p. 159.

6. Jacques Derrida, *Writing and Difference,* trans. Alan Bass (Chicago: University of Chicago Press, 1978), p. 67.

7. *Writing,* p. 74.

8. Arnold Schoenberg, *Moses and Aaron,* trans. Allen Forte (New York: Columbia Records M 233594).

9. *Grammatology,* p. 98.

10. Grammatology, p. 71.

11. *Writing,* p. 114.

12. *Writing,* p. 297.

13. *Writing,* p. 296.

14. *Grammatology,* p. 93.

15. *Grammatology,* p. 10.

16. *Grammatology,* p. 283.

17. Robert P. Scharlemann, *The Being of God* (New York: Seabury Press, 1981), p. 130.

18. Mircea Eliade, *No Souvenirs,* trans. Fred H. Johnson, Jr. (New York: Harper & Row, 1977), p. 74.

19. Eliade, p. 67.

20. Jean-Paul Sartre, *Nausea,* trans. Lloyd Alexander (New York: New Directions, 1959), p. 173.

21. Sartre, p. 176.

22. Marcel Proust, *The Past Recaptured,* trans. Andreas Mayor (New York: Random House, 1970), p. 129.

23. Proust, p. 131.

24. Proust, pp. 133 f.

25. Proust, p. 134.

26. Proust, p. 132.

27. Ranier Maria Rilke, *Duino Elegies,* trans. J. B. Leishman and Stephen Spender (New York: W. W. Norton, 1939), pp. 72f.

28. Rilke, pp. 74f.

29. G. W. F. Hegel, *Phenomenology of Spirit,* trans. A. V. Miller (Oxford: Clarendon Press, 1977), p. 27.

Contributors

THOMAS J. J. ALTIZER is Professor of English and Religious Studies at the State University of New York at Stony Brook and author of *Descent into Hell, The Self-Embodiment of God,* and *Total Presence.*

MAX A. MYERS is Chairperson of the Department of Theology, St. Bonaventure University.

CARL RASCHKE is Associate Professor of Religious Studies at the University of Denver and author of *The Alchemy of the Word* and *The Interruption of Eternity.*

ROBERT P. SCHARLEMANN is Comonwealth Professor of Religious Studies at the University of Virginia and author of *Reflection and Doubt in the Thought of Paul Tillich* and *The Being of God: Theology and the Experience of Truth.*

MARK C. TAYLOR is Professor of Religion at Williams College, Williamstown, Massachusetts, and author of *Kierkegaard's Pseudonymous Authorship: A Study of Time and the Self, Religion and the Human Image,* and *Journeys to Selfhood: Hegel and Kierkegaard.*

CHARLES E. WINQUIST is Professor of Religious Studies at the California State University at Chico and author of *The Transcendental Imagination: An Essay in Philosophical Theology, The Communion of Possibility, Homecoming: The Dynamics of Individuation,* and *Practical Hermeneutics: A Revised Agenda for the Ministry.*

178